TECHNIQUES
IN
TEACHING
WRITING

TEACHING TECHNIQUES IN ENGLISH AS A SECOND LANGUAGE
Series Editors: Russell N. Campbell and William E. Rutherford

TECHNIQUES IN TEACHING WRITING

Ann Raimes

·OXFORD UNIVERSITY PRESS·

Oxford University Press

198 Madison Avenue
New York, NY 10016 USA

Great Clarendon Street
Oxford OX2 6DP England

Oxford New York
Athens Auckland Bangkok Bogotá Buenos Aires Cape Town
Chennai Dar es Salaam Delhi Florence Hong Kong Istanbul Karachi
Kolkata Kuala Lumpur Madrid Melbourne Mexico City Mumbai Nairobi
Paris São Paulo Shanghai Singapore Taipei Tokyo Toronto Warsaw

and associated companies in
Berlin Ibadan

OXFORD is a trademark of Oxford University Press.

Library of Congress Cataloging in Publication Data
Raimes, Ann, 1938-
    Techniques in teaching writing
    (Teaching techniques in English as a second language)
    Bibliography: p.
    1. English language—Study and teaching—Foreign
speakers. I. Title. II. Series.
PE1128.A2R245 1983   808′.042   83-13096

ISBN 0-19-434131-3 (pbk.)

Copyright © 1983 by Oxford University Press

First published 1983
Printing (last digit): 20 19 18 17 16 15 14

No unauthorized photocopying.

Grateful acknowledgment is given for permission to reprint material
    from the following:
Mary Lawrence, *Writing as a Thinking Process* (Ann Arbor: University of
    Michigan Press, 1972), pp. 47, 75. Copyright © The University of
    Michigan 1972.
Martin L. Arnaudet, Mary Ellen Barrett, *Paragraph Development: A
    Guide for Students of English as a Second Language,* © 1981, pp. 14,
    48–49, 96. Reprinted by permission of Prentice-Hall, Inc., Englewood
    Cliffs, N.J.
Reprinted with permission of Macmillan Publishing Co., Inc., from *Write
    Away: A Course for Writing English as a Second Language,* Book I by
    Gloria Gallingane and Donald Byrd. Copyright © 1979 by Collier
    Macmillan International, Inc.
From *Intermediate Composition Practice, Book I,* by Linda Lonon
    Blanton. Newbury House Publishers, Rowley, Mass. 1981.
From *Elementary Anecdotes in American English* by L. A. Hill. Copyright
    ©1980 by Oxford University Press, Inc. Reprinted by permission.
D. H. Spencer, *Guided Composition Exercises,* pp. 28–29, 49–50.
    Longman, 1976.

Illustrations by Steven Schindler.
Graphics by Andrew Mudryk.

Printed in China

To my mother,
HILDA POPE

·EDITORS' PREFACE·

It has been apparent for some time that little attention has been given to the needs of practicing and student teachers of English as a Second Language.* Although numerous inservice and pre-service teacher-training programs are offered throughout the world, these often suffer for lack of appropriate instructional materials. Seldom are books written that present practical information that relates directly to daily classroom instruction. What teachers want are useful ideas, suggestions, demonstrations, and examples of teaching techniques that have proven successful in the classroom—techniques that are consistent with established theoretical principles and that others in our profession have found to be expedient, practical, and relevant to the real-life circumstances in which most teachers work.

It was in recognition of this need that we began our search for scholars in our field who had distinguished themselves in particular instructional aspects of second language teaching. We sought out those who had been especially successful in communicating to their colleagues the characteristics of language teaching and testing techniques that have been found to be appropriate for students from elementary school through college and adult education programs. We also sought in those same scholars evidence of an awareness and understanding of current theories of language learning together with the ability to translate the essence of a theory into practical applications for the classroom.

*In this volume, and in others in the series, we have chosen to use *English as a Second Language (ESL)* to refer to English teaching in the United States (as a second language) *as well as* English teaching in other countries (as a foreign language).

Our search has been successful. For this volume, as well as for others in this series, we have chosen a colleague who is extraordinarily competent and exceedingly willing to share with practicing teachers the considerable knowledge that she has gained from many years of experience.

Professor Raimes' book is devoted entirely to the presentation and exemplification of practical techniques in the teaching of writing. Each chapter of her book contains, in addition to detailed consideration of a wide variety of techniques, a number of activities that teachers can perform that tie the content of the book directly to the teachers' responsibilities in their classes. With this volume then, a critical need in the language teaching field has been met.

We are extremely pleased to join with the authors in this series and with Oxford University Press in making these books available to our fellow teachers. We are confident that the books will enable language teachers around the world to increase their effectiveness while at the same time making their task an easier and more enjoyable one.

Russell N. Campbell
William E. Rutherford

Editors' Note: Apologies are made for the generalized use of the masculine pronoun. It is meant to be used for simplicity's sake, rather than to indicate a philosophical viewpoint. We feel that the *s/he, her/him, his/her* forms, while they may be philosophically appealing, are confusing.

·ACKNOWLEDGMENTS·

Many of the ideas in this book have evolved from conversations with my colleagues in our offices and at professional meetings. Thanks go in particular to Ann Berthoff of the University of Massachusetts, whose trenchant insights into a philosophy of teaching writing have so often influenced my own thinking. Margot Gramer of Oxford University Press, and the editors of this volume, Russell Campbell and William Rutherford, have all responded to my writing and offered many helpful suggestions. I owe special thanks to those who suffered with me through the drafts, blocks, and revisions of the writing process—my family: James, Emily, and Lucy Raimes. Their unfailing support and sense of balance helped me make time for writing and reminded me when it was time to stop and do other things.

·CONTENTS·

TECHNIQUES
IN
TEACHING
WRITING

·CHAPTER ONE·

INTRODUCTION: TEACHING WRITING IN ESL CLASSES

When we learn a second language, we learn to communicate with other people: to understand them, talk to them, read what they have written and write to them. An integral part of participating fully in a new cultural setting is learning how to communicate when the other person is not right there in front of us, listening to our words and looking at our gestures and facial expressions. Visitors to another country will often have to leave a note for the mailman, fill out a customs declaration form, give written instructions, or write a thank-you letter.

But the fact that people frequently have to communicate with each other in writing is not the only reason to include writing as a part of our second-language syllabus. There is an additional and very important reason: writing helps our students learn. How? First, writing reinforces the grammatical structures, idioms, and vocabulary that we have been teaching our students. Second, when our students write, they also have a chance to be adventurous with the language, to go beyond what they have just learned to say, to take risks. Third, when they write, they necessarily become very involved with the new language; the effort to express ideas and the constant use of eye, hand, and brain is a unique way to reinforce learning.[1] As writers struggle with what to put down next or how to put it down on paper, they often discover something new to write or a new way of expressing their idea. They discover a real need for finding the right word and the right sentence. The close relationship between writing and thinking makes writing a valuable part of any language course.

A great deal of writing that goes on in ESL lessons, especially in an elementary-level class, is sentence writing. Students repeat or complete given sentences to reinforce the structure, grammar, and vocabulary they have learned. They work with pattern sentences, performing substitutions or transformations. This book will concentrate on techniques to get students to go beyond those sentence exercises, so that they write

- to communicate with a reader;
- to express ideas without the pressure of face-to-face communication;
- to explore a subject;
- to record experience;
- to become familiar with the conventions of written English discourse (a text).

SPEAKING AND WRITING

Some of you may wonder why it is not enough to teach our students how to speak English adequately: won't they then obviously be able to write it? Not necessarily, for writing is not simply speech written down on paper. Learning to write is not just a "natural" extension of learning to speak a language. We learned to speak our first language at home without systematic instruction, whereas most of us had to be taught in school how to write that same language. Many adult native speakers of a language find writing difficult. The two processes, speaking and writing, are not identical.

Let us look at some of the differences between writing and speaking:

1. Speech is universal; everyone acquires a native language in the first few years of life. Not everyone learns to read and write.
2. The spoken language has dialect variations. The written language generally demands standard forms of grammar, syntax, and vocabulary.
3. Speakers use their voices (pitch, stress, and rhythm) and bod-

ies (gestures and facial expressions) to help convey their ideas. Writers have to rely on the words on the page to express their meaning.

4. Speakers use pauses and intonation. Writers use punctuation.

5. Speakers pronounce. Writers spell.

6. Speaking is usually spontaneous and unplanned. Most writing takes time. It is planned. We can go back and change what we have written.

7. A speaker speaks to a listener who is right there, nodding or frowning, interrupting or questioning. For the writer, the reader's response is either delayed or nonexistent. The writer has only that one chance to convey information and be interesting and accurate enough to hold the reader's attention.

8. Speech is usually informal and repetitive. We say things like, "What I mean is . . ." or "Let me start again." Writing, on the other hand, is more formal and compact. It progresses logically with fewer digressions and explanations.

9. Speakers use simple sentences connected by a lot of **and**'s and **but**'s. Writers use more complex sentences, with connecting words like **however, who,** and **in addition.** While we could easily *say*, "His father runs ten miles every day and is very healthy," we might well *write*, "His father, who runs ten miles every day, is very healthy."

When we look at just these few differences—and there are many more—we can see that our students will not just "pick up" writing as they learn other skills in ESL classes. We have to teach writing. And that, of course, leads to the next question and the subject of this book: How?

APPROACHES TO TEACHING WRITING IN ESL CLASSES

There is no one answer to the question of how to teach writing in ESL classes. There are as many answers as there are teachers and teaching styles, or learners and learning styles. The following diagram shows *what* writers have to deal with as they produce a piece of writing:

Producing a Piece of Writing

SNYTAX
sentence structure,
sentence boundaries,
stylistic choices, *etc.*

CONTENT
relevance, clarity,
originality,
logic, *etc.*

GRAMMAR
rules for verbs,
agreement, articles,
pronouns, *etc.*

THE WRITER'S
PROCESS
getting ideas,
getting started,
writing drafts,
revising

MECHANICS
handwriting,
spelling,
punctuation, *etc.*

Clear, fluent, and effective communication of ideas

AUDIENCE
the reader/s

ORGANIZATION
paragraphs,
topic and support,
cohesion and unity

WORD CHOICE
vocabulary,
idiom, tone

PURPOSE
the reason for writing

As teachers have stressed different features of the diagram, combining them with *how* they think writing is learned, they have developed a variety of approaches to the teaching of writing.

The Controlled-to-Free Approach

In the 1950s and early 1960s, the audio-lingual approach dominated second-language learning. Speech was primary and writing served to reinforce speech in that it stressed mastery of grammatical and syntactic forms. ESL teachers developed techniques to move students towards this mastery. The controlled-to-free approach in writing is sequential: students are first given sentence exercises, then paragraphs to copy or manipulate grammatically by, for instance, changing questions to statements, present to past, or plural to singular. They might also change words or clauses or combine sentences. They work on given material and perform strictly prescribed operations on it.[2] With these controlled compositions, it is relatively easy for students to write a great deal yet avoid errors. Because the students have a limited opportunity to make mistakes, the teacher's job of marking papers is quick and easy. Only after reaching a high intermediate or advanced level of proficiency are students allowed to try some free compositions, in which they express their own ideas. This approach stresses three features of the diagram above: grammar, syntax, and mechanics. It emphasizes accuracy rather than fluency or originality.

The Free-Writing Approach

Some teachers and researchers have stressed quantity of writing rather than quality. They have, that is, approached the teaching of writing by assigning vast amounts of free writing on given topics, with only minimal correction of error. The emphasis in this approach is that intermediate-level students should put content and fluency first and not worry about form.[3] Once ideas are down on the page, grammatical accuracy, organization, and the rest will gradually follow.

To emphasize fluency even more, some ESL teachers begin many of their classes by asking students to write freely on any topic without worrying about grammar and spelling for five or ten minutes. At first, students find this very difficult. They have to resort to writing sentences like, "I can't think of anything to write." As they do this kind of writing more and more often, however, some find that they write more fluently and that putting words down on paper is not so frightening after all. The teachers do not correct these short pieces of free writing; they simply read them and perhaps comment on the ideas the writer expressed. Alternatively, some students might volunteer to read their own aloud to the class. Concern for "audience" and "content" are seen as important in this approach, especially since the free writings often revolve around subjects that the students are interested in, and those subjects then become the basis for other more focused writing tasks.

The Paragraph-Pattern Approach

Instead of accuracy of grammar or fluency of content, the paragraph-pattern approach stresses another feature of the diagram on page 6, organization. Students copy paragraphs, analyze the form of model paragraphs, and imitate model passages. They put scrambled sentences into paragraph order, they identify general and specific statements, they choose or invent an appropriate topic sentence, they insert or delete sentences. This approach is based on the principle that in different cultures people construct and organize their communication with each other in different ways. So even if students organize their ideas well in their first language, they still need to see, analyze, and practice the particularly "English" features of a piece of writing.[4]

The Grammar-Syntax-Organization Approach

Some teachers have stressed the need to work simultaneously on more than one of the features in the composition diagram. Writing, they say, cannot be seen as composed of separate skills which are learned one by one. So they devise writing tasks that lead students to pay attention to organization while they also work on the necessary grammar and syntax. For instance, to write a clear set of instructions on how to operate a calculator, the writer needs more than the appropriate vocabulary. He needs the simple forms of verbs; an organizational plan based on chronology; sequence words like **first, then, finally**; and perhaps even sentence structures like "When . . . , then . . ." During discussion and preparation of the task, all these are reviewed or taught for the first time. Students see the connection between what they are trying to write and what they need to write it. This approach, then, links the purpose of a piece of writing to the forms that are needed to convey the message.[5]

The Communicative Approach

The communicative approach stresses the purpose of a piece of writing and the audience for it. Student writers are encouraged to behave like writers in real life and to ask themselves the crucial questions about purpose and audience:

- Why am I writing this?
- Who will read it?

Traditionally, the teacher alone has been the audience for student writing. But some feel that writers do their best when writing is truly a communicative act, with a writer writing for a real reader.[6] Teachers using the communicative approach, therefore, have extended the readership. They extend it to other students in the class, who not only read the piece but actually do something with it, such as respond, rewrite in another form, summarize, or make comments—but not correct. Or the teachers specify readers outside the classroom, thus providing student writers with a context in which to select appropriate content, language, and levels of formality. "Describe your room at home" is not merely an exercise in the use of the present tense and in prepositions. The task takes on new dimensions when the assignment reads:

- You are writing to a pen pal (in an English-speaking country) and telling him or her about your room. You like your room, so you want to make it sound as attractive as possible.

or

- You are writing to your pen pal's mother and telling her about your room. You do not like your room much at the moment and you want to make changes, so you want your pen pal's mother to "see" what is wrong with your room.

or

- You are participating in a student exchange program with another school. Students will exchange schools and homes for three months. A blind student whom you have never written to before will be coming to your home and occupying your room. Describe the room in detail so that that student will be able to picture it, imagining that your description will then be read onto tape so that the student can listen to it.

Real classroom readers can be brought into these assignments, too, if students role play, exchange letters, and write back to each other, asking questions and making comments.

The Process Approach

Recently, the teaching of writing has begun to move away from a concentration on the written product to an emphasis on the process of writing. Writers ask themselves not only questions about purpose and audience, but also the crucial questions:

How do I write this? How do I get started?

All writers make decisions on how to begin and how to organize the task. Student writers in particular need to realize that what they first put down on paper is not necessarily their finished product but just a beginning, a setting out of the first ideas, a draft. They should not expect that the words they put on paper will be perfect right away. A student who is given the time for the process to work, along with the appropriate feedback from readers such as the teacher or other students, will discover new ideas, new sentences, and new words as he plans, writes a first draft, and revises what he has written for a second draft. Many teachers in ESL classes now give their students the opportunity to explore a topic fully in such prewriting activities as discussion, reading, debate, brainstorming, and list making. (Throughout the book, I use the word **brainstorming** to mean producing words, phrases, ideas as rapidly as possible, just as they occur to us, without concern for appropriateness, order, or accuracy. As we produce free associations, we make connections and generate ideas. Brainstorming can be done out loud in a class or group, or individually on paper.) The first piece of writing produced is not corrected or graded. The reader responds only to the ideas expressed.

So in the process approach, the students do not write on a given topic in a restricted time and hand in the composition for the teacher to "correct"—which usually means to find the errors. Rather, they explore a topic through writing, showing the teacher and each other their drafts, and using what they write to read over, think about, and move them on to new ideas.

Teachers who use the process approach give their students two crucial supports: *time* for the students to try out ideas and *feedback* on the content of what they write in their drafts. They find that then the writing process becomes a process of discovery for the students: discovery of new ideas and new language forms to express those ideas.[7]

APPROACHES AND TECHNIQUES

All of the approaches just mentioned do, of course, overlap. We will seldom find a classroom where a teacher is so devoted to one approach as to exclude all others. A teacher using a communicative or a process approach will still use techniques drawn from other approaches as the students need them; model paragraphs, controlled compositions, free writing, sentence exercises, and paragraph analysis are useful in all approaches. Just as most teachers and textbooks are eclectic—drawing from everything that is available to them—this book, too, will not limit itself to techniques derived solely from one approach. There is no *one* way to teach writing, but many ways. Nor will this book limit itself to any specific features of the composition diagram on page 6. But although the techniques are drawn from all approaches and address the various features that a writer needs to consider in producing a piece of writing, they still have something in common. They stem from the basic assumptions that writing means writing a connected text and not just single sentences, that writers write for a purpose and a reader, and that the process of writing is a valuable learning tool for all of our students.

·CHAPTER TWO·

TECHNIQUES IN PLANNING THE CLASS: SEVEN BASIC QUESTIONS

Choosing classroom techniques is the day-to-day business of every writing teacher. Any decision we make—such as whether to provide students with a first sentence or not, or whether to mark all errors or only a selected few—is a decision about a teaching technique. The variety of techniques available to teachers nowadays in textbooks and training courses can be bewildering. Examining them with some basic questions in mind will help us sort out which ones suit our class, our student level, and the approach that underlies our own curriculum and our own teaching. These questions are not confined to any one of the approaches outlined in the last chapter; whichever approach you as a teacher personally favor, these questions can be a help to you in making your daily decision of what to do in the next class.

QUESTION 1:

How Can Writing Help My Students Learn Their Second Language Better?

While writing and the process of struggling with language to get ideas down on paper is a valuable aid to the whole learning process, it should not be singled out as though it exists in a vacuum. There is rarely a situation in real life in which we do not talk to someone or read something at some point in our writing process, before we write, while we are engaged in writing, or after we have written. When students complain, as they often do, about how difficult it is to write in a second language, they are talking not only about the difficulty of "finding" the right words and using the correct grammar but about the difficulty of finding and expressing *ideas* in a new language. For them the problem is with communicating and not just with writing.

Finding and communicating ideas is not encouraged by the typical textbook task of writing about a subject in class or at home and then handing in the finished composition to a teacher who points out the errors. There is a better way. Instead, we can take the same textbook topic but build in class activities that will help prepare students for the assignment and give them the opportunity to speak, listen to, read, and write the new language in the process of making and communicating their meaning.

For example, the topic "Describe the best places for a tourist to visit in your home town" can be dealt with in the following ways to provide communicative practice in all the language skills to help students generate ideas (prewriting) and revise those ideas (rewriting):

• Discuss with the class a possible audience for this piece of writing, for example, "You are writing a brochure for a travel agency to attract foreign visitors to your home town. Which two places would you recommend?"

• Students make lists of the places they would mention in the brochure.

• In groups, students compare their lists and discuss why they included specific places. Each group then makes a composite list of places to include.

• Each group selects from the list the two places they would recommend most highly.

• Each group reports to the whole class on which two places the students chose, and why. The teacher or another student summarizes the discussion on the board, thus putting relevant vocabulary and idioms right in front of the students' eyes.

• Now the students write a draft of a description for the brochure.

• They read each other's papers and compare their descriptions with those of other students in the group; they discuss which one is the most effective and why.

• The person in charge of the brochure wants to have two

descriptions to choose from. All the students put the first piece of writing away and tackle the assignment again. This rewriting is not, therefore, just copying the first draft and making a few minor corrections.

• They proofread carefully. Then they exchange papers and the partner checks the paper for clarity of ideas and then for spelling, punctuation, and grammar.

In this way, classroom activity in a writing lesson can engage the students in a variety of language use that goes beyond the usual sequence of teacher giving directions, students writing, and teacher marking. Students can also be actively engaged with all the language skills even while doing controlled writing exercises. We can, for instance, ask student groups to discuss a punctuation fill-in exercise, present oral explanations of their choices, and read the group's finished product aloud.

A writing lesson need not, therefore, take place in a heads-down, silent classroom. For any task, we should consider what classroom activities will help our students use the new language in a meaningful way so that speaking it, listening to it, and reading it help them write it with more confidence.

QUESTION 2:

How Can I Find Enough Topics?

In all my twenty years as a teacher, observing teachers and working with them, I have been struck time and time again by how hard ESL writing teachers work. They think up a topic or search through the textbook to find one, ask students to write about it, mark all the papers, and then much too quickly move on and think up another topic. A good topic is seldom explored beyond the one composition that students write. What a waste that is! The longer students grapple with a subject, the more their command of the necessary vocabulary and idiom develops; the more they read on the topic, the more they learn about organizational structure and sentence structure; the more they discuss a topic, the more ideas they develop. Our problem isn't really finding enough topics; it's developing enough tasks from the good topics we have.

Unfortunately, good topics are not always plentiful. One useful source that is often overlooked is the students themselves and their interests. We find out about these from class discussion, from questionnaires, or when we ask the students to write daily notes or to do ten-minute in-class free writing. Wherever we originally get a topic—from students, from a book, or from our own invention—the first thing we should consider is not which one assignment will be best but how many assignments we can develop so that our students can explore the subject as fully as possible. A reading passage, a controlled composition, a sentence-combining exercise, scrambled sentences to organize into a paragraph, a dictation, a lecture, role-playing activities, a passage to copy, a letter to write, a form to fill out, or a graph to interpret—all of these can emerge from the same topic instead of one being about space travel and another about John and Mary's picnic. As the students do the tasks we assign, they thus learn both about the new language and about the subject the language is dealing with. So for us, finding enough topics means finding a few excellent topics of interest to students and building a whole series of assignments around them.

QUESTION 3:

How Can I Help to Make the Subject Matter Meaningful?

If we ask all our students to practice chronological order by writing an account of a fictional Mai Ling's daily routine by using the information in a list like:

    7:00 a.m. gets up
    8:00 a.m. has breakfast
    etc.

we know, don't we, that as we read our students' compositions we will not be very interested in *what* they are writing but rather in *how* they are writing it and whether their spelling and grammar are accurate. But it is easy to make the same type of task much more interesting and meaningful. If, for instance, only half the students in the class have the list of Mai Ling's activities in front of them, there is then an "information gap" in the classroom.[1] Those with the lists know something that others do not. When they write to those without the lists, they are therefore telling them something that they did not know before. Students who read the completed written account can respond by trying to reconstruct the original list that provided the information. Or, students can write for each other (or for the teacher) about their own daily routine; the reader is then reading totally new and original subject matter.

The reader certainly needs to find the subject matter of a piece of writing interesting, but even before that, the writer needs to be interested in the task. It therefore needs a purpose to it other than just "language practice." Of course, personal topics (autobiography, family biography, pastimes, preferences, problems) always permit real information to be conveyed. But when topics move away from personal narrative, students find it helpful if we specify a communicative purpose for each piece of writing, not just, "Write a composition telling why you would like a new bicycle" but, "You have entered a competition to win a new bicycle. The winner will be the one who writes the most convincing reasons why he or she wants that bicycle. Try to win the competition." The same principle applies to guided and controlled writing. The assignment to write a paragraph beginning with the sentence "A beach vacation is always relaxing" is only writing practice. The assignment to "Write an advertisement for a beach resort and try to convince people to take a beach vacation instead of traveling abroad" gives the task more meaning for the writer. Consider also such directions as: "Change the verbs in the following passage to the past tense. Make any other changes necessary." The directions are clear, but they leave a student wondering if in English it is an entirely arbitrary matter whether we use present or past tense! Better directions would be: "The passage below contains a description of the daily activities of a man who is being watched by the police. You are a detective who observed the suspect yesterday. Write an account for your boss of what the suspect did."

So with every task that we assign our students, we should consider how to make it as meaningful as possible for both the reader and the writer. The writer will put more thought and effort into a piece of writing that communicates his own interests and opinions to a reader, and a reader, whether the teacher or another student, will certainly be able to respond to a piece of writing if he or she is made interested in the content. The subject matter of the topics should, as far as possible, involve writers and readers in the communication of real meaning.

QUESTION 4:

Who Will Read What My Students Write?

Traditionally, the teacher has been not so much the reader as the judge of students' writing. Teachers correct errors in grammar and spelling, they make evaluative comments like "Very good" or "Could be improved," and they rewrite the students' muddled sentences. Students have therefore seen writing as something where what they say is less important than the fact that the grammar and syntax follow the rules.

One problem that arises from this is that student writers rarely see that their writing is a piece of reading for someone else—a piece that should be clear and interesting to the reader. The presence of a reader—a real reader, that is, and not a judge—helps the writer establish the goal of his writing: communication with that reader. For each writing task, we should specify one or more of the following readers:

1. the teacher, helping in the process by reading and commenting on drafts and not correcting errors until a predetermined point in the process, as distinct from the teacher as test-giver and evaluator, judging and marking the final product;

2. one other student in the class, exchanging a draft with the writer and commenting on the draft he reads;

3. a group of students in the class, reading a draft or listening to it read aloud and commenting on it;

4. a real outside audience: such a reader is addressed by, for example, a letter to a student travel organization, a class magazine of student writing, writing samples displayed on a bulletin board, a letter to a pen pal, or a description of a national custom for a school in another country. My daughter's school regularly receives descriptions of Japanese customs and events—written in English by a class of eight-year-old children in Japan—and displays the descriptions on bulletin boards for all the English-speaking children to read in their study of Japan;

5. an imaginary outside audience: with this type of reader, students engage in a simulation game, a role-playing activity in writing. Pretending that they are in a specific situation, they write for a specific reader, as in: "You are a landscape architect. Write a description for the city council of how you will design the new city park." In most cases, the real readers will, of course, be the students or the teacher. As readers they, too, can role-play and respond to the piece of writing as a member of the city council might respond;

6. the student himself, writing a poem, a few notes, or a draft for his eyes alone.

Ensuring that the students know whom they are writing for is an important step in the planning of any class.

QUESTION 5:

How Are the Students Going to Work Together in the Classroom?

Once we have established topics, purpose, audience, and some integrated language activities, we have to think of our actual class time and what directions we will give the students. Will they work together as a class, in groups, in pairs, or individually? Will they write in class or at home? How will the class actually proceed once the subject matter for writing has been introduced?

Group work in the classroom has been shown to be valuable for native speakers who are learning to write.[2] Inexperienced writers are less fearful when a few of their peers read and comment on what they write; they like to see what their peers produce, and they welcome the unthreatening exchange of ideas that happens in a small group. For second-language learners, who need more time and opportunity to practice using the language with others, group work is especially beneficial. The problem is that the teacher might justifiably feel that with groups of students talking to each other, away from the teacher's direct supervision, a little of the teacher's control of the class is sacrificed. To some extent, it probably is. But when control means that it is mostly the teacher who is speaking and asking questions, we have to realize how drastically student participation and involvement drops. The students, not the teacher, need the practice in language use. Our planning should take that into account.

Consider the following two situations:

1. You assign a writing topic, such as "My Favorite Sport," to your students, tell them how to go about doing it, explain what you want in a piece of writing, and give them thirty minutes to write the composition. Or you assign a controlled composition in which students complete sentences in a paragraph about José's favorite sport.

2. You ask a question, such as "What is your favorite sport and why?" and ask students to discuss this in the class in small groups of four or five students. During the discussion, you walk around the room, contributing to the groups' discussions, helping students who are stuck for particular words or phrases, and asking leading questions to draw more silent students into the discussion. One student in each group takes notes and keeps an account of the discussion and later reports to the whole class so that other students can comment and ask questions. While each group is reporting to the whole class, a student writes a summary of the main points on the board. Only then do the students write—for a student in another group as the reader.

In the first writing situation, students listen to the teacher and then plunge into the writing. They are entirely dependent upon their own resources, for both content and grammar, with no access to any sources of information. In the second situation, students begin by actually using—before they write—the content, vocabulary, idiom, grammar, and sentence structure that they will need when they do write. They rehearse the topic, they get ideas from hearing others, they make connections. When they finally sit down to write, the blank page is no longer quite so awesome.

Before we start a lesson, it is useful for us to decide exactly how we will set up the classroom and structure the activities. If we decide that working in pairs or small groups will be beneficial, then we also have to decide whether to select the pairs or groups ourselves or to let the students do that. Here we have to take into account the personalities, abilities, and preferences of the students. Sometimes it is useful to establish a group leader, one who directs the operations of the group and ensures that only English is spoken. While it is good to plan like this, we also have to be flexible. If a pair or group of students do not work well together, we have to be prepared to adapt our plan: perhaps a whole-class discussion, with all the students and the teacher sitting in a circle, gives the more talkative students a chance to have their say in front of a large audience so that afterwards, in groups, the less vocal students continue and comment on the whole-class discussion.

Group work can be as beneficial to the teacher as it is to the students. A small group of students can collaborate in the process of writing, for instance, a letter of inquiry to a Tourist Information Office. They all agree on the format and wording and all write out the agreed-upon version. The teacher, however, collects only one version from each group to comment on. Later, the students in each group discuss the teacher's comments on their piece of writing and revise it accordingly.[3] Thus the students benefit by helping each other with vocabulary, syntax, content, and organization and by doing a lot of speaking and listening to each other, and the teacher benefits by cutting down on the number of compositions he collects.

It is important to remember while planning a writing lesson that while writing is often an individual activity, it does not always have to be so in the classroom. Students can interact with each other at all points in the process: before they write, while they are writing, and after they have written.

QUESTION 6:

How Much Time Should I Give My Students for Their Writing?

Obviously, a lot of language activities and group work take a lot more time than the usual writing assignment. Before we can assess how much time to allow for a writing task, we have to examine what writers actually do when they write. Here are activities that a lot of writers say they do, though not necessarily all of these, and certainly not always in this order:

- They identify why they are writing;
- They identify whom they are writing for;
- They gather material through observing, brainstorming, making notes or lists, talking to others, and reading;
- They plan how to go about the task and how to organize the material;
- They write a draft;
- They read the draft critically;
- They revise;
- They prepare more drafts and then a final version;
- They proofread for errors.

These procedures do not, of course, occur in a step-by-step linear fashion. Even as we write a draft, we might change our plan, rewrite sections, or alter our intended audience. What is clear from our examination of what writers actually do is that time is a crucial element in the writing process and an element that distinguishes writing from speaking. Writers have time to make decisions, time to play around with ideas, time to construct and reconstruct sentences, to form and re-form arguments, to experiment with new words, and above all, time to change their minds. Time should not be a constraint, and revision should not be a punishment for the writer (as in "You have made six mistakes; please rewrite the composition") but a built-in part of the writing process.

So when we plan our curriculum, it is important for us to include enough time for students to explore a topic thoroughly and to try again. Students need to be encouraged to write "messy" notes, to scribble ideas, to tear up what they have written and to start again. Only in that way will they be able to make their writing more interesting, organized, and accurate.

QUESTION 7:

What Do I Do About Errors?

Our principal job as teachers of composition is not to search for errors—that, after all, is what our students should be doing before they hand in their papers to us. But obviously, when our ESL students write, they do make a lot of mistakes and it becomes necessary for us to devise ways of dealing with the errors so that they do not become the sole focus of the piece of writing. A specific assignment will call for its own schedule and method of error correction. Some general strategies for all assignments follow.

• See errors as friends and not as enemies to be conquered; they tell you a great deal about your students and their learning processes, for in errors we can see evidence of the learning process at work.

• Use errors in students' writing to plan ahead: What do the students need to work on next? What are they having trouble with?

• Give your students time and opportunity to correct errors before you do. Find out if they *can* correct: Was the error due to carelessness, lack of application of a learned rule in this new context, or lack of knowledge of a structure? Establishing the causes of errors can be helpful to us and to our students.

• If your students are producing notes, lists, or a first draft, concentrate on meaning. Question only the really major errors, like jumbled sentences, which interfere with communication so much that you can't work out what the student is trying to say. Let the students, with your help, identify and correct all the other errors later. This is difficult for teachers to do. Most of us automatically reach for a pen or pencil as soon as we pick up a piece of student writing, so we have to train ourselves to read without a pen in our hand and to consider what ideas the writer has tried to express.

- Devise a system for indicating some or all of the errors in the student's second or third draft. Explain the system to the students, along with the follow-up procedures that you expect.
- Learn to expect errors that occur regularly at certain stages in a student's learning development. For instance, after learning the past tense forms of regular verbs, students will tend to over-generalize and produce forms like **bringed** and **cutted**. View these as signs of learning rather than as unforgivable errors.

· ACTIVITIES ·

1. If you are using an ESL textbook in your class, take any one topic for writing from it and ask yourself the seven questions about how you will plan the activities of a series of lessons around that topic. If you are not using a textbook, take any one topic that you have assigned or might assign to a class. Discuss with other teachers your responses to the seven questions.

2. With the map on the opposite page as a topic, how many different types of writing tasks can you develop? Try to include skills other than writing, to use small groups in the classroom, and to provide students with the opportunity to convey real information and to respond to each other's work.

3. Rewrite the following composition topic—"A Person I Admire"—so that you are more specific about
a. the purpose of the piece of writing
b. the audience for the piece of writing
c. directions to lead students through the writing process.

Then write the assignment yourself. What errors do you think your students might make in this assignment? How can you help the students avoid or find and correct those errors?

4. How could the picture on page 70 be used in a writing class so that:
a. the students provide other students with real information— that is, how can the picture be used to provide an "information gap" in the classroom?
b. the students work in groups?

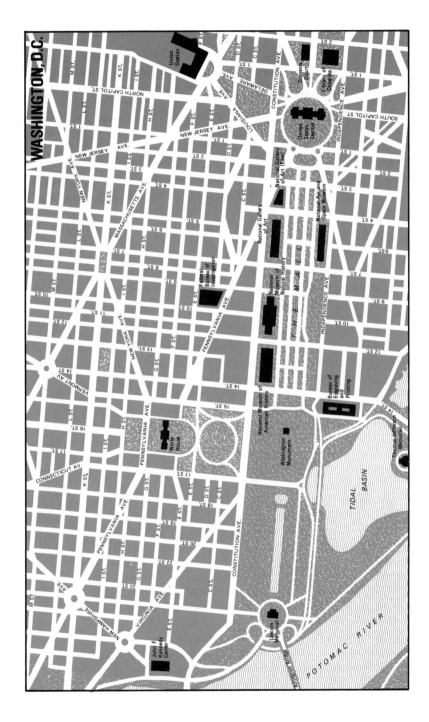

5. The next time you write something in either your native language or a second language, observe what you do. Make notes about your own process. Discuss your process—and your problems—with other teachers. Note any similarities to or differences from the list of activities on page 21.

6. Your students were interested to read about a young man from the United States, unemployed and in and out of mental hospitals, who sued his parents for bringing him up badly and not giving him a good start in life. You decide to have the class explore the topic of the influence of parents on children.

a. Devise as many materials as you can for writing lessons based on this topic. Explain how the materials would be used in the classroom.

b. Write instructions for a specific composition assignment and include directions for prewriting activities in groups and for the writing and rewriting of drafts.

c. Examine the composition assignment you invented in (b) above and try to predict what this assignment will demand in terms of vocabulary, grammar, syntax, and organization. How will you prepare the students for these demands?

·CHAPTER THREE·

TECHNIQUES IN USING PICTURES

All ESL writing teachers can find a valuable resource in pictures: drawings, photographs, posters, slides, cartoons, magazine advertisements, diagrams, graphs, tables, charts, and maps. First of all, pictures provide a shared experience for students in the class, a common base that leads to a variety of language activities. When students write about a personal topic like "My most frightening experience," the material is not shared. It comes from any and all of their experience. Beyond predicting the use of the past tense, there is little that the teacher can do to prepare a whole class to deal with the vocabulary and sentence patterns that the writers will need. With a picture, however, all students, after close observation of the material, will immediately need the appropriate vocabulary, idiom, and sentence structure to discuss what they see. So pictures are valuable, too, in that they provide for the use of a common vocabulary and common language forms. In addition, a picture can be the basis for not just one task but many, ranging from fairly mechanical controlled compositions, sentence-combining exercises, or sequencing of sentences to the writing of original dialogs, letters, reports, or essays. A whole series of connected activities can be generated from the source of one picture. Finally, because everybody likes to look at pictures, their use in the classroom provides a stimulating focus for students' attention. Pictures bring the outside world into the classroom in a vividly concrete way. So a picture is a valuable resource as it provides:

1. a shared experience in the classroom;
2. a need for common language forms to use in the classroom;
3. a variety of tasks;
4. a focus of interest for students.

THE USE OF PICTURES IN THE CLASSROOM

Before we examine in detail how to use some actual pictures in a classroom, some suggestions for general strategies for using any pictures might be useful:

1. Whole-class discussion, which then leads to writing, can be generated by many types of pictures, such as posters, textbook pictures, magazine pictures pasted onto stiff cardboard and displayed at the front of the room, simple pictures drawn on the blackboard, or duplicated drawings.

2. To provide a student audience for student writers, give half the class one picture, the other half another. A range of communicative tasks for small groups opens up now, with students conveying real information to others.

3. With students working in pairs or small groups, give each student of the pair or give each group a different picture to work with. This frees you from the necessity of obtaining class sets of pictures. It also provides students with a real communicative task. When a few students have the only copy of a picture, it is then necessary for them to be able to inform the rest of the class about it.

4. Real communicative tasks can be developed by using in the classroom pictures that the students themselves provide. There is a double advantage here: the teacher is relieved of the task of finding a picture and the students have something that has personal meaning for them to answer questions about and write about in the classroom. Students can be asked to provide their favorite advertisements, their own drawings, a reproduction of their favorite work of art, or a family photograph.

5. Do not limit classroom work to what the students can actually see in the picture. Remember that students can make inferences, predictions, and suppositions about the world beyond the frame of the picture. Ask the students to use their imagination to visualize what happened just before the moment in the picture and what will happen next, or to infer what caused the situation presented in the figures in the chart and what the result will be.

ONE PICTURE—MANY DIFFERENT TECHNIQUES

Let us look now at what we can do in the classroom with one simple sketch. The one below is representative of the type we often find in textbooks or can draw on the board ourselves. Even if we don't think of ourselves as artists, most of us can manage to sketch a living room, a bedroom, an apartment floor plan, or a simple map. We do not have to produce an inspired or interesting picture; the point here is to use any simple picture to gen-

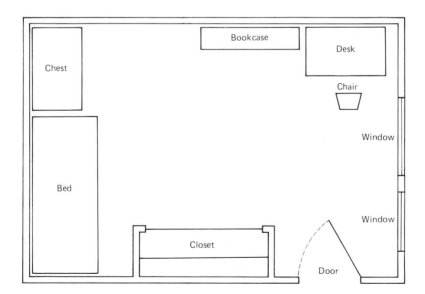

erate interesting activities that go beyond the mundane one of "Describe the picture." The following activities, based on a sketch of an American bedroom (you can, of course, vary the sketch or change the room), are suggestions for classroom techniques that teachers can choose from. They are not intended to be a series of sequential exercises.

Examples

1. Description

Draw the diagram (unlabeled) on the board. The students write down words that could be used to label the items in the room drawn. Class discussion should provide consensus on how to label the diagram. Then, in small groups, students discuss and write down what other words and phrases they will need in order to describe the room, e.g., **next to, on the left,** etc. The teacher now erases the diagram from the board and the students write a description of the room from their memory. They exchange papers and draw the diagram of the room their partner has described.

2. Description, comparison, and contrast

a. Divide the class into pairs of students and give the picture to Student 1 of each pair, who writes a description of it for Student 2. (It might be useful first to review with the whole class the use of the present tense, the use of **there is** and **there are**, prepositions of place, and any new vocabulary words.) From the written description he receives, Student 2 tries to draw a sketch of the room.

b. While Student 1 is writing about the picture, Student 2 writes a description of a room that he knows well. He gives the description to Student 1, who then tries to draw a labeled sketch of the room and the furniture.

c. The two students look at the two sketches and the two descriptions and make lists of the similarities and differences between the two rooms. Together they write, for the rest of the class, a composition that points out these similarities and differences. Before they begin to write, they discuss how to organize the material they have in their lists.

3. Paragraph assembly

Prepare index cards with one sentence on each, which together form a paragraph about the picture. Use the passage in (5) on page 32. Hand out one index card to each pair or small group of students. The task for the whole class is to put the sentences on the cards in order so that they form a paragraph. When asked, "Who has a sentence that could be the first sentence of the paragraph?" we expect to hear from the students with "Debbie Johnson's bedroom in her home in Catskill is small but practical" rather than from those with "It is next to the door."

4. Sentence combining

Index cards can be used as in example (3) above, with the information on the cards separated so that each card contains a sentence that combines with another to make a new sentence. For example, two cards, given to two students, might read:

- Debbie Johnson's room is small.

and

- Debbie Johnson's room is practical.

Each student finds a partner whose sentence will combine with the one he has. (This part of the lesson involves quite a lot of noise and action as students move around the room searching for a partner.) Once the students have found a partner, they consider the options of how to combine the two ideas to make one sentence. Some of the possibilities with the two sentences above are:

- Debbie Johnson's room is small $\begin{Bmatrix} \text{and} \\ \text{but} \\ \text{yet} \end{Bmatrix}$ practical.
- Although Debbie Johnson's room is small, it is practical.
- Though small, Debbie Johnson's room is practical.
- Debbie Johnson's room, $\begin{Bmatrix} \text{though} \\ \text{while} \end{Bmatrix}$ small, is practical.

With the new sentences they have formed, the students can now discuss how to organize those sentences to make a paragraph, as in (3) above.

5. Paragraph completion

Prepare a paragraph about the picture and write it on the board but omit the ending (in brackets).

> Debbie Johnson's bedroom in her home in Catskill is small but practical. The room is only 10′ × 14′, but the furniture is conveniently placed. As you walk through the door, you see the desk on the right side of the long wall. To the left of the desk, there is a bookcase with four shelves. In the far left corner of the room, there is a chest of drawers. The rest of the short wall on the left is occupied by the bed. Then, on the wall next to the bed [there is a big closet with two shelves and space to hang clothes. It is next to the door. On the right-hand wall there are two windows, which make the room very light and airy.]

The students discuss how to end the paragraph. Then they compare their versions with each other's and with the version above.

6. Controlled composition

Ask the students to pretend that they are Debbie Johnson. She is now sixty years old and is writing to a grandchild to describe her room in her old family house in Catskill. The students rewrite the paragraph in (5) above, using the past tense: "My bedroom was small. . . ."

7. Guided composition

Ask the students to discuss in small groups what they would write in a paragraph beginning with:

> • Debbie Johnson's room in her home in Catskill is very colorful.
>
> *or*
>
> • Debbie Johnson's room in her home in Catskill is very drab.

They list all the details they would include, imagining the colors, curtains, ornaments, wall and floor coverings, and bed cover. Then the students in the group write a paragraph together, including details that develop the idea in the first sentence.

8. Role-play
Ask the students, in pairs or groups, to imagine that the diagram shows a room at a summer sports camp. They are working for the camp's advertising agency and have to prepare a brochure to attract young people to the summer sports camp. Their boss has asked them to begin with: "Every youngster who comes to Waterside Camp has an extremely attractive private room." They have a meeting to discuss what details should be included. Then they write a paragraph. They all read their own aloud to each other and discuss which one works the best, and why.

9. Questions and answers
a. Divide the students into groups of four. Give each student in the group a card with a word on it, for example, **bed, desk, closet**. Tell them that they have been invited to go to the United States to live with the Johnson family in their private house in Catskill, and they want to know about the room they will live in. The groups compile questions about the items on their cards.

Collect the questions from each group and redistribute them to other groups. Each group of students now writes a letter from Debbie Johnson that gives answers to the questions asked.

b. If students need a great deal of guidance with their writing, questions and answers can be used in the following way:
Give the students a list of questions.
- Does the picture show a living room or a bedroom?
- Is the room large or small?
- Is the room well organized or badly organized?

They write answers in complete sentences; when they put those sentences together, they will form a paragraph. As they do this, they can be led into some sentence combining such as suggested in (4).

10. Beyond the picture
Students look at a plan of a room (the one above, or one produced by a student or the teacher) and discuss what the other rooms in the house might look like. Each group produces a plan and a description of a different room in the house. Together, these make up a description of a whole house.

ONE PICTURE—A SEQUENCE OF TASKS

Using a picture as a topic for several writing classes gives us the opportunity to develop not merely a wide variety of tasks but also a sequence of tasks, carefully selected so that students move from one level of difficulty to another, gathering more vocabulary, knowledge of idiom and sentence structure, and organizational skill as they proceed. The picture can be used as a reference point for students to discuss a cultural phenomenon and their own experience related to it. The picture below could, for example, be used as the basis for a variety of sequential tasks.

Fred Reuss/Photo Researchers. Reprinted by permission.

Examples

1. In groups, the students discuss the answer to the question, "What is happening in the picture?" They write down words and phrases that they use. The groups compare their results. The teacher writes the necessary vocabulary on the board: wedding, marriage, get married, bride, groom, husband, wife, fiancé, reception, ceremony, etc.

2. In groups again, students discuss the answers to such questions as:

- How old are the two people getting married?
- Do their parents want them to get married?
- What jobs do the two people have?
- Will the couple have children? When? How many?
- Have you ever been to a wedding? Was it like this one?

The groups report to the whole class the results of the discussion. The teacher writes necessary vocabulary words and idioms on the board.

3. The class reads a paragraph describing Debbie Johnson's traditional wedding:

> Debbie Johnson and Frank Willett had a traditional wedding last Saturday. The bride wore her grandmother's veil and her mother's wedding dress, which was made of white satin. She wore her sister's necklace and carried a bouquet of blue flowers—so she had the bride's traditional "something old, something new, something borrowed, something blue." She had six bridesmaids. They wore long dresses of flowered blue lace. The bridegroom and the bride's father were wearing traditional morning suits—a black jacket and gray pants. The couple were married in church and the bride's parents held a reception for 100 guests at their home.

The students examine the paragraph and determine which sentence makes the main point. Then they list the details the writer includes to show the reader why he can make that point.

4. The students imagine that they are Debbie Johnson writing a letter to a friend abroad, six months before the wedding, telling her what the wedding will be like. They rewrite the paragraph above, using the future tense with **will**, making all necessary changes, and beginning with:

> My dear Lucy,
>
> In six months Frank and I will be getting married! Here are our plans for the wedding. I will wear my grandmother's veil and ...

The task is to make the letter as realistic as possible, so the students will have more to do than just change the verbs. **The couple** will become **we, the bride's parents** will become **my parents,** and so on.

5. Small groups of students discuss and write a description of the wedding in the picture above for a local newspaper. They read these descriptions aloud and write them on the board. Other students make comments and suggestions.

6. The students now, after discussion, write to a group of American students to describe a typical traditional wedding in their country.

PICTURE SETS

Pairs of pictures or pictures in sequence provide for a variety of guided and free writing exercises. A picture sequence, such as a comic strip, provides the subject matter for writing narrative and for speculating about the story beyond the pictures in the strip. A set of parallel pictures—pictures that show a similar scene or tell a similar story—provides material that offers guidance on vocabulary, sentence structure, and organization yet lets the students write about new subject matter.

Examples

1. The students individually write a list of sentences about a picture sequence (see below) frame by frame, for example: "Betty left work at 5 o'clock. It was raining." Then in small groups, they work on combining or linking the sentences to make continuous prose, such as "When Betty left work at 5 o'clock, it was raining, so she ..."[1]

2. The whole class works with the picture sequence, but with the pictures out of order. In small groups, the students discuss which order is correct for the pictures, and why. Then they write the story of the pictures.[2]

3. One group is given only two of the pictures in the sequence, while another group receives the other two. The groups discuss and write what they think the four-picture sequence shows. They exchange papers and read each other's. Only then do they show each other their two pictures.

4. The students are given cards, each containing a separate sentence which describes the picture below: "There is a candy store on the corner." "The candy store is open."

Then they match sentences to parts of the picture and arrange the sentences in order. Then the students are given a parallel picture, such as the one below.

In groups, they use the paragraph they have just assembled to write a parallel paragraph about the parallel picture.[3] Both the first picture and the sentences describing it serve as a model for the new piece of writing.

5. A more advanced class can use the same pictures as above, but now the students discuss the first picture and write their own description of it, either in groups or as a whole-class activity. They read their descriptions aloud and discuss them. Then the students write about the parallel picture, using their own writing as a model.

DIAGRAMS, TABLES, GRAPHS, AND CHARTS

Especially effective communicative tasks can be derived from diagrams, tables, graphs, and charts. Students deal with given information presented visually, and they work on conveying the same information in writing, that is, in a letter, report, or composition. The limits of the task are thus immediately controlled by the type of information presented; the students invent their own sentences but do not have to invent the material. They therefore work within strict limits of vocabulary and content. If the teacher gives the visual material to only half the class or to only one student of a pair, then when the students write to each other to convey the information, the need for clarity, coherence, and completeness becomes obvious, particularly when the student receiving the written information has to process it and present it again in its original form.

Examples
1. Give a different line diagram to each student in a pair, for example:

Each one writes instructions on how to draw the diagram. The students exchange the written instructions, follow them, and try to re-create the diagram. Then they look at the original diagram and compare it to their own version and discuss how inaccuracies occurred. Such a task can also be tied in to the subjects of other

courses that the students might be taking. Students can, for
example, be asked to write instructions on how to set up an
experiment or how to draw the position of the planets.

2. Give each student in a pair a table, either Table A or B:

Table A

State	Square Miles	Population
New York	49,576	17,557,288
New Jersey	7,836	7,364,158
Pennsylvania	45,333	11,866,728

Table B

State	Square Miles	Population[4]
California	158,693	23,668,562
Nevada	110,540	799,184
Oregon	96,981	2,632,663

The students write about the three states in their table, including
the figures, for example: "Nevada, with 110,540 square miles, is
bigger than Oregon, with 96,981 square miles. Yet . . ." Then the
students exchange papers and reproduce the original table from
which the paragraph was written. Class discussion follows on
which state they chose to write about first, second, and last, why
they made that choice, and whether they made any comparisons.

3. Give students a model of a family tree, perhaps your own, a
famous person's, or one that you invent:

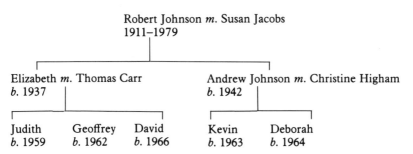

Ask students to draw as much as they can of their family tree. Then they write a letter to a genealogist, including all the information contained in the tree diagram. Another student reads the description and reconstructs the family tree from it.

4. Students fill out the following chart about who does the jobs in their home:

Member of family?   **Job**
                                         cleans the house
                                         makes the beds
                                         cleans your room
                                         looks after the plants or garden
                                         looks after the animals
                                         prepares breakfast
                                         cooks dinner
                                         washes dishes
                                         washes clothes
                                         does repairs
                                         pays the bills
                                         paints and decorates the house[5]

Then they exchange charts with a partner and use the information on the new chart to write a paragraph. Ask the students to begin with a sentence that makes a generalization about the details on the chart, for example, "Anwar's mother does most of the household jobs."

MAPS

Maps are a valuable resource in the language-learning classroom. Not only do they provide a visual framework for the use of language skills, but they also provide real information about the country whose language the students are studying. With large-scale maps of sections of cities, street maps of small towns, as well as maps of states and countries, students can practice giving directions and using the words and syntax that describe spatial relationships.

Examples

1. Draw a street map on the board. Then give students cards containing sentences with information about the buildings, monuments, parks, etc. One card should contain information about location:

- The Empire State Building is on the corner of Fifth Avenue and 34th Street.

Others give a description:

- The Empire State Building has a wonderful view.
- The Empire State Building has 102 floors.

Using their cards, the students first identify and then describe the places marked on the map. Then the whole class assembles all the given sentences into a logical paragraph for a tourist taking a walking tour.[6]

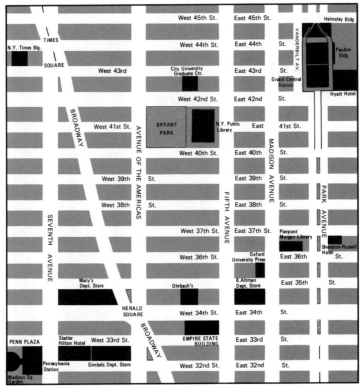

2. Students look at two maps of different states such as the ones below. They read a paragraph about one of the states. They then write a parallel paragraph about the other state for a travel brochure, using the information on the map.

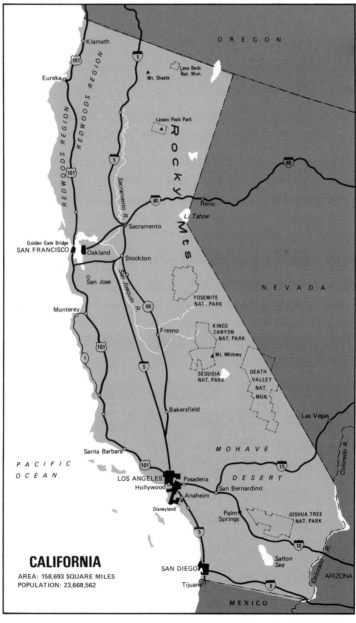

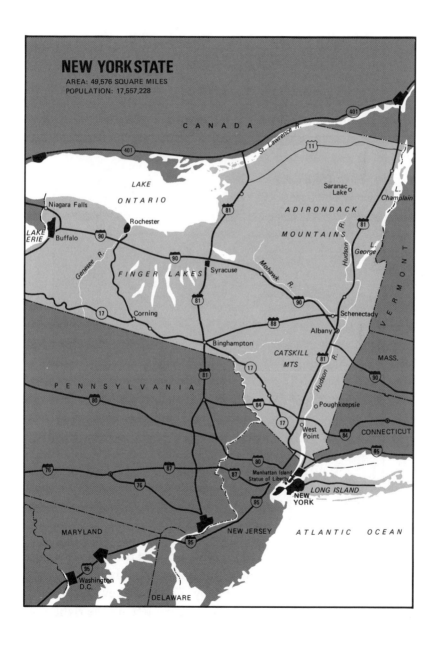

California, which covers 158,693 square miles, has a population of 23,668,562. It joins the Pacific Ocean, and it is bordered by Oregon, Nevada, Arizona, and Mexico. The capital city is Sacramento, and the other major cities are San Francisco and Los Angeles. There are a lot of tourist attractions in the state of California: the redwood forests, Yosemite National Park, and, of course, Disneyland.

3. All the students have the same map:

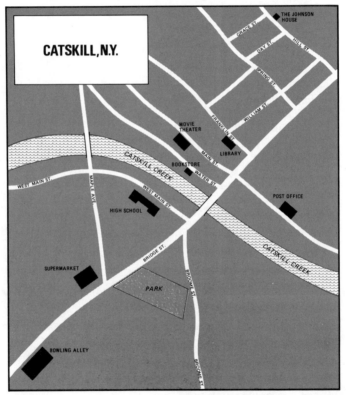

In groups, the students write directions for how to get from Debbie Johnson's house in Catskill, New York, to the post office, the movie theater, the bookstore, the park, the high school, the supermarket, and the bowling alley. For this, they will need to help each other with expressions like **turn left, on the right**, and **straight ahead**.

·ACTIVITIES·

1. Use the photo below to:

a. devise a guided assignment for a low intermediate class, with a clearly expressed purpose and audience;

b. write a passage for a controlled composition exercise. Give clear directions for the changes the students are to make. Tell them why and for whom they are writing.

Jim Kalett/Photo Researchers. From *People and Crowds*, p. 70. Copyright © by Dover Publications, Inc.

2. a. How many writing activities can you devise from this graph? Write the directions for the students.

Tanta, Egypt; Jidda, Saudi Arabia; Kuwait, Kuwait; Basra, Iraq; and El Paso, Texas in the United States of America, have something in common. They all have a very small amount of rain each year. The graph below shows how much rain each city gets in a year.

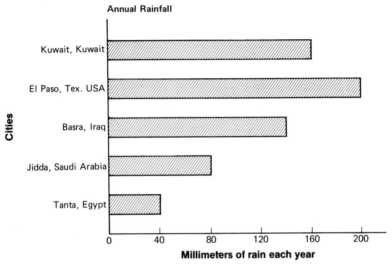

Source: Frank Ebos and Timothy Howell, *Mathematics: Problem Solving Activities.* Boston: Houghton Mifflin, 1978, p. 29. Reprinted by permission of the publisher.

b. Write a paragraph about the graph and from it prepare instructions for a paragraph-assembly exercise and for a sentence-combining exercise.

c. Devise a writing task which would lead students to use expressions like **more than, less than, the most, the least, next to the most,** etc. Write the instructions for the students.

3. Find a picture in a textbook or magazine, or draw a picture yourself. Discuss with other teachers what words and idioms the students will need in order to write about the picture and what writing activities could be generated by this picture. List them.

4. Using the picture on page 104, prepare materials and a lesson plan based on three of the following:
• a role-playing activity;

- a controlled composition;
- a piece of writing that communicates real information to someone in the class;
- a paragraph-assembly exercise.

Discuss also how you would sequence the activities you chose.

5. Find a set of pictures, such as a comic strip. Write instructions for students for two writing activities based on the set of pictures. Be specific about who will read what the students write.

6. Use the map of Washington, D.C., on page 25 to:
a. prepare sentences for a paragraph-assembly exercise;
b. write instructions for students for a writing task in which they have to write directions on how to get from one place to another. Establish a purpose and an audience for the piece of writing.

·CHAPTER FOUR·

TECHNIQUES
IN USING
READINGS

A short story, a newspaper column, an advertisement, a letter, a magazine article, a poem, or a piece of student writing can work the same way as a picture to provide shared content in the classroom. Readings can also, like pictures, be used to create an information gap that leads to communicative activities: if the students work with a variety of readings at the same time, then they will be dealing with different content, and anything they write to each other will thus be authentic communication, conveying new and real information.

However, readings can do far more in the teaching of writing than simply provide subject matter for discussion and for composition topics. When our students read, they engage actively with the new language and culture. If they are studying English where they have little opportunity to speak it or hear it spoken, then reading is the only activity that gives them access to unlimited amounts of the language. The more our students read, the more they become familiar with the vocabulary, idiom, sentence patterns, organizational flow, and cultural assumptions of native speakers of the language.

As well as learning a lot about the language and culture in general, students who read interact with a text that somebody else has written, so they can learn a great deal about writing, too. From close reading of a text, they see what one writer chose to do with the content. They have direct access to the product of a native speaker of the language and they can return to this product again and again.

There are two types of reading we can ask our students to do: extensive reading or close reading. They can read whole stories or whole books, where they have so much to read that they cannot stop to look up every unfamiliar word or to translate every sentence. They then have such a lot of reading to get through, at a level that is challenging for them—a little above the level of the language they themselves produce—that they have to read for content, for meaning. Or, we can ask our students to do close reading, where they read a short passage and give close attention to all the choices the writer has made in, for example, content, vocabulary, and organization.

Obviously, any reading the students do relates to writing in that what they read was once written. When they read professional writing, they interact with the finished product. When students read each other's writing, the product is not perfect; the advantage is that students can intervene in the process, questioning, commenting on, and supporting each other's work in progress. The activities we can ask students to do in the classroom to tie their reading in with their writing fall into two broad categories: they can work either with the text or from the text. Students work with the text when they copy and when they examine the writer's choices of specific linguistic and logical features, such as cohesive links, punctuation, grammar, sentence arrangement, and organization. They work from the text when they use it to create a text of their own, that is, when they summarize, complete, speculate, or react.

The techniques that follow include activities for working with and from a text. The use of a reading passage to examine a writer's organization is not, however, dealt with in detail in this chapter but in Chapter 8, "Techniques in Teaching Organization."

COPY

Copying is frequently used as a technique with elementary-level students. It gives practice with mastering what might be a new alphabet, moving the hand on the page from left to right, and developing fluency of handwriting.[1] It gives all students practice with the mechanics of punctuation, spelling, capitalization, and paragraph indentation.

But there is a problem with copying and that is how to make it a meaningful activity. If students see copying merely as a tedious exercise, they will lose interest and eventually make mistakes out of boredom. When do people in the real world outside the language classroom make a copy? When they want to save or remember something, like an address, a recipe, a quotation, or a poem. In the classroom, we can make copying useful if we ask our students to copy down some information that they will then really use. So if we have only a limited number of copies of a reading passage, we can turn this to advantage by having students write out the passage for a partner. Then the copy is actually read and actually used. There is a real reason for the copier to try to make it accurate.

Copying can be integrated with other classroom activities in a variety of ways.

Examples

1. After small-group discussion of specific questions about a story or dialog, each group writes on the board exactly what answers the group produced. All the students in the class copy these answers, so that they assemble a variety of ideas in their notebooks before they begin to plan and organize their own response to the dialog or story.

2. A good piece of writing by one student is written on the board and then all the students copy it down as a model. Later a student can use that same copied passage to read to the class for practice in dictation or summary writing.

3. Students read a story at home and copy out the one sentence they like best. Then, in class, all the students discuss the choice.

4. The production of a class magazine, or even just of a few samples of writing, provides numerous opportunities for students to copy their own or other students' writing so that it is legible and error free.

5. During class discussion of a reading, the teacher writes new

vocabulary words on the board. The students keep a vocabulary notebook or vocabulary notecards; they copy any new words into the book or onto the cards, and write a sentence for each new word. They thus compile a personal dictionary or vocabulary list.

EXAMINE COHESIVE LINKS

When students examine a piece of writing closely, they can make discoveries about the devices the writer has used to connect one sentence to another in order to make the text cohesive. Writing a text, a connected piece, is different from writing a series of sentences in an exercise. In a text, there are logical and linguistic links between the sentences. Learning how to use these links is an important part of learning how to write a language. (An example of this is in my last sentence, where the word **these** connects the word **links** to the same word in the previous sentence.) Students need to learn about the devices that make a text cohesive; such devices include some ESL troublespots like personal pronouns and adjectives, demonstrative pronouns and adjectives, the definite article, and connecting words.[2]

Connecting words, in particular, cause problems. When students have been speaking in class and speaking for the most part in single sentences, they have no familiarity with the connecting words that are so necessary in a piece of writing. These are the words and phrases that we use to add an idea (such as **also, in addition, furthermore**), to show sequence (**first, then, after that, next, finally**), to show result (**so, therefore, as a result, consequently**), and to show contrast (**but, however, nevertheless, on the other hand**). So our students need to be made aware of how these connecting words are used in a piece of writing.

Examples

1. Students read a passage, with all the pronouns and possessive adjectives circled. Then they draw a line to connect the circled words to the words they refer to:

A boy, about ten years old, appeared at a third-floor window. It wouldn't open. He was very frightened. . . .

They can now do the same with their own or each other's writing.

2. In a reading passage, the students replace all the circled words with the words they refer to, as in Example 1: "The window wouldn't open. The boy was very frightened." Then they discuss why a writer would choose to use the pronoun forms.

3. Students read a passage and circle the instances of **the.** Then they determine in which cases **the** provides a link to a noun that has been mentioned before:

> A boy appeared at a third-floor window. (The) boy was very frightened. He broke (the) window and then. . . .

4. Ask your students to find a reading passage in their textbook and copy it out but leave blanks for any connecting words. Then the papers are passed on to other students in the class who fill in the connecting words. (The letter on page 110 would be a suitable passage for such an exercise, in which the students would delete the words **first, second, third,** and **finally.**)

5. Give your students a text with the linking words deleted:

> When I think of my father, I think of 1____ at meal-times. 2____, 3____ always sat at the head of the family table and asked 4____ children a lot of questions. He asked us about 5____ friends and our day at school. He was disappointed when he heard about any difficulties or failures in school. 6____, he never got angry.

In groups, students try to fill in the blanks from their knowledge of English and the sense they can make of the passage. Then students are given a list of words, with the writer's actual choice included:

1. man   him*   only   everyone
2. often   fat   then*   finally
3. he*   she   we   father
4. all   their   naughty   his*
5. our*   many   much   valuable
6. in addition   therefore   although   however*

They discuss which word the writer used and compare it with the word they originally chose. Then they can work on examining the pronoun links and drawing lines to show connections, as in Example 1 above.

EXAMINE PUNCTUATION AND GRAMMAR

When students examine a piece of writing closely, they can make discoveries not only about the cohesive devices the writer uses but also about the rules of punctuation and grammar that the writer employs. Close reading of a short passage lets the students scrutinize the choices the writer has made and the rules he has followed. This consideration of choices and rules is important at any level of writing ability. An elementary-level student might wonder whether to write two short sentences or whether to combine them with a comma and the word **and.** A more advanced writer wonders if he can begin a sentence with a word ending in **-ing.** Students of all levels can benefit from reading a text and identifying and describing the grammatical rules used in it. Students who have previously written only single sentences for grammatical practice need to be particularly aware of how punctuation is used in a longer text. They will not learn it in their spoken English practice, for punctuation is a feature only of the written language. It is helpful for students to examine where and how writers use commas, semicolons, colons, and exclamation marks and to derive rules from examining the punctuation on the printed page.

Examples

1. Give students a short passage, such as the one on page 58, and ask them, in groups, to discuss and explain why each punctuation mark is used. Or give them a passage with all the punctuation marks omitted. The students' task is now to fill in the punctuation. If students do this task in groups and are encouraged to produce just one final version for each group, they will become involved in discussion and will even argue about where commas belong, and why.

2. Ask students to examine a piece of writing for any grammatical feature that they are having difficulty with. They might, for example, look for all the **-ed** endings and categorize them as past tense endings, participle endings in a verb phrase, or participle endings in an adjective phrase. Or, with a short passage or even with just a few sentences like the ones below, the students make a chart of the **-s** endings: Is the **-s** a part of the stem of the word, a noun ending, a verb ending, a contraction, or a possessive?[3]

> She takes a bus and then walks three miles to her daughter's school. She's been doing this for four years.
>
> **−s as part of a word**
>
> bu*s*   thi*s*
>
> **Noun + plural** *−s*
>
> mile *−s*   year *−s*
>
> **Verb + singular** *−s*
>
> take *−s*   walk *−s*
>
> **Possessive** *−'s*
>
> daughter'*s*
>
> **Contraction** *−'s* **(is, has)**
>
> she'*s* (=**she has**)

EXAMINE SENTENCE ARRANGEMENT

Very often, students of English as a Second Language will write a series of sentences that are accurate grammatically if we look at each sentence in isolation; however, the sentences do not seem to "hang together" very well. One student, for example, wrote these three sentences:

> (1) Our house had four bedrooms and two sitting rooms. (2) A large garden was in front of the house. (3) My father had planted a lot of flowers in the garden.

A first step towards improving this piece of writing was to make the sentences fit together better:

(1) Our house had four bedrooms and two sitting rooms. (2) In front of the house was a large garden. (3) In the garden my father had planted a lot of flowers.[4]

Our students need to examine a text carefully to find out if the sentences hang together according to the basic principle that old information comes before new information in a sentence. In Sentence 2, **the house** is old information, as it was referred to previously in Sentence 1; **a large garden** is the new information. What students need here is a lot of practice in making choices within a text between sentences that convey the same meaning as individual sentences, but are arranged differently.

Examples

1. Give students a sentence, followed by two sentences—both with the same meaning—that could follow it. The students discuss the alternatives and make a choice, explaining the reason for the choice:

a. When I arrived at the house, my mother was sitting in her rocking chair.
Choose which sentence follows:

- This chair was given to my mother when I was born.
- When I was born, someone gave my mother this chair.

b. Every four years we have what we call leap year.
Choose which sentence follows:

- The month of February has 29 days in a leap year.
- In a leap year, the month of February has 29 days.

2. Give students two sentences with a gap between them and a choice of sentences to fill the gap. The students discuss which sentence is the best one to fill the gap, and why:

After only a few hours, the snow in a city street becomes soft and dirty. _____.
Slush makes our feet wet, our streets ugly, and our children miserable because they can't throw snowballs any more!

Choose one sentence to put in the gap:

- The name of this soft, dirty snow is slush.
- Slush is what this soft, dirty snow is called.
- This soft, dirty snow is called slush.

3. Take any short, simple reading passage and examine the sentences, with the students deciding what information in each sentence is old and what is new.

SUMMARIZE

Summarizing provides students with valuable practice in searching for meaning and communicating that meaning. Faced with a reading passage, they have not only to find out what the main ideas are but also to be able to express them in their own words. This ability of the language learner to understand concepts, process them, and restate them in his own words is a major goal of the language-learning process.

Examples

1. Divide the class into six groups, each with about five students. Create an information gap by giving each group a different reading passage—a story or dialog—to work with. Each member of the group writes a summary of their passage for another group. The students within the group discuss their summaries and choose the best one to give to another group. Members of the group receiving the summary ask additional questions about the reading passage if they need clarification. Finally, members of the first group copy out the whole story and give it to the second group. After they have done this on a few occasions with passages assigned by the teacher, they then summarize each other's writing. The challenge then is: Can the reader spot the writer's main point? Is that main point clearly expressed? Is it as clear to the reader as it is to the writer?

2. Students read the following passage:

> When the fire engine left the fire station on Hicks
> Street at 8:00 p.m. on Saturday, the fireman Bill Ros-

coe did not know that he would return a hero. Flames were leaping out of a first-floor window of the corner house on Livingston Street. Neighbors, police, and firemen stood outside on the sidewalk. Suddenly they all looked up and shouted as they heard a scream. A boy, about ten years old, appeared at a third-floor window. It wouldn't open. He was very frightened. Bill Roscoe dropped the hose, stepped forward, jumped, and grabbed the bottom rung of the metal fire escape ladder. Then he climbed up to the window, broke it, pulled the boy out of the window and carried him down the ladder. Both were safe, and the crowd cheered.

Then they turn the page over, and write a one-sentence summary of the passage. They choose which of the following sentences best summarizes the passage and compare it with the sentence they wrote:

a. The writer talks about how dangerous a fire can be.
b. The writer warns families not to leave children alone in the house.
c. The writer describes the brave act of the fireman.

3. Students read a short newspaper article, such as the one above, and consider which parts of the article they would print if they were the newspaper editor and had space in the paper for only a few sentences. The students are thus being asked which parts express the main idea of the piece of writing.

4. When students are reading extensively to gain more familiarity with their new language, it is helpful if they write a few sentences summarizing a short story, an essay, or a chapter. This task makes them distill and communicate the content; it makes them realize that they will not be held responsible for understanding, remembering, and recording every single detail. What they are reading for is the meaning of the whole piece. Students who are reading the same story can later compare their summaries to see if they agree on what the main points are.

COMPLETE

When students examine a reading passage with parts (words, phrases, sentences, or larger chunks) missing, they have to consider a great many features of writing if they are to complete it. Obviously they have to consider meaning and the grammatical and syntactic fit of the part they add. In addition, they have to put themselves in the position of the writer and then tone, style, and organization become important. A piece of writing with an informal tone would not be likely to suddenly switch to a formal tone; a narrative would not usually develop into a philosophical argument. Completion exercises ask students to discern the original writer's purpose, audience, and personal style and to pay attention to those in the completed version.

Examples

1. Give out the article about the fireman (page 58) but with the first or last sentence missing or both. The students write sentences which might be appropriate to complete the paragraph. They discuss and compare their choices.

2. Give students the entire paragraph about the fireman, and give them some additional information that the newspaper reporter now wants to add to the article. The students have to decide where they will fit the new information into the article and whether any changes need to be made in the wording.[5]

- The fireman swung his legs up and got his feet in place.
- The crowds thought the house was empty, so they were quite calm.

3. Give the students a passage to read which stops at words like **however, and so,** or **and then:**

The sun was shining and there were no clouds in the sky when Jane left her house to go to the beach. However, . . .

The students discuss what might come next in the story and then they complete the story.

4. A grammar completion exercise can precede, provide the subject matter for, and lead up to a free writing exercise. Students are given a passage with, for example, the verbs removed; in groups they discuss which verb and form belongs in each blank space:

> When I ＿＿ two years old, I ＿＿ an elephant for the
> first time. This ＿＿ in Atlantic City in New Jersey.
> While my parents were ＿＿ on the beach, I ＿＿
> them and ＿＿ along the beach. Suddenly, right in
> front of me, ＿＿ a building in the shape of an ele-
> phant. I couldn't ＿＿ my eyes! "Look, entu!" I ＿＿.
> I had not yet ＿＿ how to say the word **elephant.**

Verbs:

wander	stand	believe
be	learn	happen
leave	sit	shout
see		

After the completion exercise, students discuss an early childhood memory of their own. Then they write about it for the classroom bulletin board, using the past tense and beginning with, "When I was ＿＿ years old. . . ."

SPECULATE

Speculation involves thinking beyond the given text. Speculative questions open up opportunities for both discussion and writing. Just look at the number of such questions that can be asked about the straightforward passage on pp. 58–59. Why was the boy alone in the house? What does a fireman do every day? How would the boy describe the event in a letter to his grandmother? What letter would the owner of the house write to the insurance company? What precautions should everyone take to prevent fire at home? How would the boy describe the incident? Would you like to be a fireman/-woman? Why or why not? Many of these can be used as topics for discussion and writing. In addition to speculation beyond the given text, students can be given tasks that encourage them to speculate about the text itself, about its content, context, organization, and the writer's choices of words and syntax.

Examples

1. Students read the article about the fireman on pp. 58–59 and speculate about how the little boy's mother, who was not at home when the fire occurred, might have reacted. They make a list of her reactions on the blackboard. Then they write a letter from the boy's mother to the fireman.

2. Prepare index cards with the following roles written on them:

> the fireman
> the little boy
> the owner of the building
> a passer-by
> a next-door neighbor

Duplicate the roles as many times as necessary for the number of students in your class. Distribute one card to each student. The students form groups (all the "firemen" together, etc.) and discuss how the fire would have affected them in their role. Then they write a letter to the newspaper after the article about the fire appeared and they describe the fire in detail from the point of view of the person on their card.

3. Just one sentence can spark a great deal of speculation. Using a short passage from your textbook, give students only the first sentence of a paragraph or the first sentence of each of a series of paragraphs. The students discuss and try to predict what the rest of the text might contain. The students use those first sentences to speculate about both content and form, for example: "This paragraph will tell a story; the next paragraph will tell us why the writer thinks that his math teacher is the best in the world." The students can write their own versions of the paragraphs and then compare them to the original passage. Student writing can be used to similar effect. One student's first line is discussed by others: "What do you expect to read in a piece of writing that begins like this?" The students write their versions of what they expect and then compare these to the student's original version.

4. A good way to interest students in reading some stories in their second language is to give them a list of the first lines of well-known and readily available stories and novels, such as:
• It was a bright cold day in April and the clocks were striking thirteen. (George Orwell, *1984*)
• The great fish moved silently through the night water, propelled by short sweeps of its crescent tail. (Peter Benchley, *Jaws*)
• One dollar and eighty-seven cents. That was all. And sixty cents of it was in pennies. (O. Henry, "The Gift of the Magi")

The students discuss which story they would like to read and why. They discuss what they can guess about the content of the story. With an advanced class, the teacher might then ask the students to read the book they chose.

5. In a classroom activity similar to but rather more structured than the preceding one, the students read only the first paragraph of a reading passage. Then the teacher gives them a choice of three sentences that might begin the second paragraph. The students discuss which sentence would fit the content, logic, organization, and grammar of the passage and what the paragraph might contain. They move through the whole passage with this kind of speculative discussion. Only at the end do they see the whole passage.

REACT

Readings help expand the world of the classroom by bringing subject matter into it. Students then have more to react to than the room, chalk, and homework. They can get interested in controversial issues, they can connect stories with their own personal experiences, and they can explore new worlds of interest. They can react to a reading assignment by discussing it, writing about it, or even by doing something active, like following directions. We can use this power of readings to generate reactions in two ways in our writing lesson: we can provide readings that stimulate the need for written communication, or we can ask our students to write (opinions, instructions, and the like) so that other students in the class have subject matter to react to.

Examples

1. Use the passage about the fireman again (page 58), but solely as a stimulus for going beyond the subject matter of the passage. Students discuss a fire they have seen, make a list of things that could start a fire, make a poster for the school warning about fire, make a poster for a child's room with three **Don't**'s on it, or write about the first three objects they would save if their house were on fire. Other students guess the authors.

2. Once students have read a passage and responded to it in writing, they have in fact provided more written material for classroom use, for students can always read what other students have written. The learner-writer finds it particularly encouraging when someone reads what he has written, understands it, and in turn responds to it. The more we can arrange classroom activities so that a piece of student writing becomes a "reading passage" not just for the teacher but for others in the class, the wider the audience the writer gets and the more he feels that what he writes and how he writes it are matters of importance. When students read each other's work, they can be asked to react by answering general questions—such as "Which part did you like best?" and "Were any parts not clear to you?"—or by following specific guidelines and identifying, for example, the one sentence that expresses the main idea of the piece of writing or the sentences that provide vivid detail.

3. Another way to react to a piece of writing is to actually do something. We read instructions and assemble a toy. We read the rules and play a new game. We receive an invitation and reply. We can create situations in the classroom by asking students to write real instructions that other students will actually carry out:

• how to draw a line diagram, such as a plan of a room (another student reads the instructions and tries to reproduce the diagram);

- how to draw a diagram of a pulley (after a science class);
- how to assemble pieces of a wooden or a paper puzzle to make specific shapes;
- how to perform a card trick.

· ACTIVITIES ·

1. In the reading passage on pp. 120–21, circle all the pronouns **these, this,** and **it** and discuss with another teacher what each word refers to. What problems might students encounter in doing such an exercise?

2. Find a reading passage in a textbook or magazine that would interest your students. Choose a passage from it that could be given to students to examine
a. cohesive links
b. punctuation and grammar.
Prepare directions for the students.

3. Use the same passage as in (2) above, and prepare a completion exercise from it by deleting words. Explain the reasons for the choice of words to delete: what will the students learn from this completion exercise?

4. Study the reading passage below:

> Pat Hogan was traveling around the country in his car. One evening he was driving along a road and looking for a small hotel when he saw an old man at the side of the road. He stopped his car and said to the old man, "I want to go to the Sun Hotel. Do you know it?"
>
> "Yes," the old man answered. "I'll show you the way."
>
> He got into Pat's car, and they drove for about

twelve miles. When they came to a small house, the old man said, "Stop here."

Pat stopped and looked at the house. "But this isn't a hotel," he said to the old man.

"No," the old man answered, "this is my house. And now I'll show you the way to the Sun Hotel. Turn around and go back nine miles. Then you'll see the Sun Hotel on the left."[6]

Discuss with another teacher how the passage could be used for writing exercises in which students speculate about the content of the text or speculate beyond the text. Write instructions for the students to work together in groups on the task.

5. Use the same passage as in (4). Devise classroom activities and write instructions for students to do meaningful writing tasks that ask them to copy and to summarize. The emphasis here is on the word *meaningful:* why are they copying and summarizing? What is the purpose? Who will read what they write?

6. How could the reading passage on page 134 be used as a basis for a piece of writing for students in which they react to the content of the reading passage? Formulate a topic for writing and describe how you would prepare the students to handle the assignment. What kinds of prewriting activities would be useful? How would you deal with the first draft? How many drafts would you expect the students to write?

7. Find a reading passage in your textbook. What writing activities are the students asked to do in connection with that reading passage? Do these activities involve working with the text or from the text? What do you think the students are supposed to learn from each of the activities?

·CHAPTER FIVE·
TECHNIQUES IN USING ALL LANGUAGE SKILLS

If we want our language learning classes to come as close as possible to real-life communicative situations, then we have to organize activities that let students use all of the language skills. In order to do this students should speak (not just repeat) and speak not only to the teacher but to each other. That means, then, that students will also listen to each other—really listen—once the classroom talk is not restricted to patterns like "Is she running? Yes, she is." With listening comes comprehending what the speaker is saying. The listener can then react by writing down for a reader his version of the information he has just heard. So we can get chains of language activity in the classroom such as this one:

- Student 1 speaks while Student 2 listens.
- Student 2 writes.
- Student 3 reads what Student 2 wrote and responds.
- Student 1 checks that 2 and 3 understood.

The value of such a sequence of activity is that it begins with the students handling the target language. Students are not just given a topic that they then immediately translate and think through in their native language before they put their ideas onto paper. Here all activities flow from what is seen and heard and the students' immediate response is in English. There is thus very little opportunity for translation.

When our students are comfortable with the normal classroom activity of using all language skills, it is up to us to ensure that they have the chance not only to use the new language but also to play with it. They need to experiment with new words and new sentence types. A pause followed by a question like "How do I say . . . ?" or "Is that word right?" should delight us, for it means that our students are taking risks with the language in their attempt to get their ideas across more effectively.

The techniques that follow are, for the most part, prewriting techniques that give students the opportunity to use all their linguistic skills to help them explore and get started with their ideas on a given topic or to allow the topic for a piece of writing to emerge out of communicative classroom activities.

BRAINSTORMING

Brainstorming lets students work together in the classroom in small groups to say as much as they can about a topic. The teacher does not have to monitor grammar or pronunciation, except when the speaker cannot be understood, though the teacher will obviously be the resource person whom students turn to as they search for the right word or the right structure to express their ideas. Whatever the writing assignment is based on—a reading, picture, map, textbook topic, personal experience, or an examination essay question—it can be preceded by student talk, specifically by a brainstorming activity, with students producing relevant vocabulary, making comments, asking questions, and making associations as freely as they can in a short time. After brainstorming orally together, students can then do the same on paper, writing down as many ideas as they can without worrying about grammar, spelling, organization, or the quality of the ideas. Then they will have something to work with, instead of a blank page.

Examples
1. Instructions to observe and talk about the picture on page 70 generated the following responses from a group of four students:

- She is probably about four years old.
- I wonder who's winning?

Photograph by Fred Plaut from *The Family of Man,* by
Edward Steichen. (New York: The Museum of Modern
Art, 1955), p. 132. Reprinted by permission of the
photographer.

- Where is her mother?
- Does her mother know she's playing with the old man?
- He's her grandfather.
- He looks like my grandfather.
- I like his face.
- She's pretty.
- What time of day do you think it is?

After about five minutes of comments and questions that arise from the free associations the students make, the group can make notes, and examine, summarize, and develop those notes to formulate a topic for a more focused discussion that will lead to a piece of writing.

2. A brainstorming session can also address a specific question, such as: "Why is the little girl playing checkers with the old man?" The students write down as much as they can as quickly as they can. Then they compare their ideas and develop them into a list.

3. Students can also be encouraged to use the brainstorming technique to help them find a topic and a direction if one is not assigned. If they keep a journal or do ten-minute writings in class, their own interests will emerge. Or if students are given a rather vague assignment of, for example, writing about a childhood memory, it might help them to think first of as many childhood memories as possible, to discuss these with others, to write them all down, and then to narrow their focus gradually so that the memory they finally decide to write about really is a vivid one that they feel others would be interested in.

GUIDED DISCUSSION

Another way to get students to talk about a topic and especially to get them to focus on specific aspects of a topic is to provide guidelines for group or whole-class discussion. The students' thinking is thus directed along predetermined lines. The ideas they come up with within the established guidelines are, however, entirely their own. If a teacher provides guidelines for discussion, that control he imposes has the advantage of letting him help the students beforehand with the vocabulary and sentence forms that they might need in their discussion.

Examples

1. Give specific directions that will guide the group in preparation for writing, for example:

a. Discuss and write down the conversation between the old man and the little girl (page 70). Include:
- greetings
- a request to play checkers
- acceptance with pleasure
- questions about age
- questions about playing checkers
- an invitation to begin the game

A review of the forms of greetings, requests, invitations, and questions would be useful here before discussion begins or during whole-class discussion.

b. Ask students to look at the picture and ask as many questions as they can about it, using the words **who, what, when, where, why,** and **how.** Then they discuss possible answers to the questions they invent and write a story about the picture.

Members of the group can be assigned roles during and after discussion:
- Discussion leader: initiates and guides discussion
- Recorder: takes notes
- Summarizer: writes a summary of the discussion
- Reporter: reports back to the whole class

2. Classroom group work for which students use all the language skills can be developed around a controlled writing exercise, too. Together students can work on a controlled composition, sentence combining, punctuating a paragraph, finding links between sentences, or sorting words into groups. All the members of the group confer on the exercise and agree on the final version. If the group has only one copy of the exercise, then the students have to sit close together to see the sheet of paper. This means that they are now close enough to talk and listen to each other. If the group is, in addition, responsible for producing just one written response with all the students' names on it, then there is pressure to reach consensus by discussion. When students doing a sentence-combining exercise argue about whether a sentence sounds better with **although** or **however,** that probably teaches them more about sentence structure and sentence variety than any number of mechanical exercises or explanations from the teacher!

INTERVIEWS

The interview is a useful technique to try with a new class so that students and teacher can get to know each other. When the students write the record of an interview, they convey to others genuine information transmitted to them by other students.

Examples

1. With an elementary class, the teacher works with the class to devise a set of questions that an interviewer might ask, such as:

- Where do you live? (Address? House or apartment?)
- Whom do you live with? (Family? Friends? Alone?)
- What do you do in your spare time?
- What are you good at? (Sports? Cooking? Skills?)
- Where do you usually go on vacation?

The students are divided into pairs and one of them is the interviewer who asks the questions and writes down answers in complete sentences. Then he arranges his sentences into a paragraph.

2. At an intermediate or advanced level, students can make up their own questions. Each student in a pair takes turns interviewing the other, making up the questions, listening to the answers, and taking notes. Then the roles are reversed and the interviewer is now interviewed. Both students write a report of the information they gathered for other students to read.

3. In a more guided interview, interviewers might be instructed to find out specific information from each other, such as how they spend their weekends, how they organize their study time, what their daily routine is like, what family meals might consist of for a typical week, or how they celebrate birthdays. Then they write a report.

4. Another way to structure the interview is to provide the interviewer with a form on which to collect information. Other students can then use that form to construct a description or a letter.

5. The teacher collects the accounts of the interviews that the pairs wrote and distributes them to other pairs of students. They might then list what questions they think the writer asked or they write more questions that they would like to know the answers to. Either way, this is good practice in writing questions! Advanced classes might combine two groups who then write a comparison/contrast of two students for the class bulletin board or magazine.

6. The students in the pair exchange their notes gathered from the interview with each other. They pretend they are reporters, writing up a report (in indirect speech) of an interview with a celebrity: "She says that she lives at . . ."

7. In pairs, students interview other teachers or students in the school, or any English-speaking adults in the community. They write a report for the classroom bulletin board, or they write a report with **X** in place of the person's name. The class has to guess who is being described.

SKITS

In a skit, the students act not as themselves but in an assigned role. This can, of course, be done either as a whole-class or a small-group activity. Writing can then follow as an outside report or summary of what was said and done or it can be a continuation of the skit, with the writers assuming the "voice" of personalities in the skit.

Examples

1. Using our example of the picture of the old man and the little girl (page 70), one group might discuss and write the dialog between grandfather and granddaughter, another the dialog between strangers who have just met each other in the park. Then both add elements from outside the picture, such as a friend of the old man's joining them, or the little girl's mother looking for her and scolding her for being home late. Then the group performs the skit, with the students playing the various parts.

Writing can then report on the skit, with students giving an account of the overheard dialog. Or it can continue the skit: the little girl's letter to a friend describing the day, the old man's diary for that day, or the little girl remembering the scene twenty years later.

2. Students can also engage in a skit developed from an event reported in the local paper. Show, for example, a diagram of a local accident involving a car and a bicycle. Divide the students into groups of three. Student 1 is the policeman, who questions Student 2, the driver of the car, and Student 3, the cyclist. Student 1 then writes an account of the accident as it was reported to him by the driver and the cyclist; Student 2 and Student 3 each write a letter to their insurance company claiming money for the damage and each placing the blame on the other.

3. With the whole class, discuss a local issue, such as a proposal to build an industrial site where the high school now stands (see map of the town of Catskill, in New York State, page 46). Discuss who might be in favor of this and who would not, and why. Distribute a card to each student or pair of students with a role specified on it: supermarket owner, a teenager, a resident of Maple Avenue, a senior citizen, an environmental specialist, or a high-school teacher. The students first discuss the issues, with reference to the town map. Then they write a skit that would represent all the roles at a town meeting. Then they write a letter to the local paper, the *Catskill Daily Mail,* expressing their approval or disapproval of the proposal and trying to win readers over to their side. Still in the same roles, they can then write replies to each other's letters.

DICTATION

The dictation technique is familiar to most ESL teachers. The teacher reads a passage through once, then reads it slowly, broken down into short, meaningful segments, which the students write down, and then the teacher reads it through once more. This gives students practice in listening carefully and paying attention to inflections and to the mechanics of spelling, punctuation, and capitalization. Frequently the teacher stands in front of the class and reads a passage which reinforces the vocabulary and grammar just taught. There are, however, alternatives to that procedure.

Examples

1. The teacher pretends to be telephoning and giving directions to get from one place to another, perhaps from a student's home to the school. As would be the case in a real telephone call of this kind, he does not give punctuation or capitals. The students write, and then compare results.

2. The teacher distributes a text with blank spaces in it:

> Oh, hello. This is _____ (who?). I tried to reach you
> _____ (when?), but you weren't home. I'm calling to
> _____ (what?) you to a party _____ (when?). There will
> be just _____ (how many?) of us, and it will be very
> informal, so you can wear _____ (what kind of?)
> clothes. Do you know my address? It's _____ (what is
> it?). I'll expect to see you at about _____ (what time?),
> then. Oh, by the way, this party is to celebrate my _____
> (what?).

Suggested answers: Jane, yesterday, invite, next Saturday, 16, casual, 16 Bridge Street, 8 o'clock, 21st birthday.

The students read it through once to themselves, then listen to the teacher read the complete passage once or twice only. Then they fill in the missing information. Of course, this activity can be done in small groups, with students helping each other with the parts they remember.

3. The teacher dictates a passage that not only gives dictation practice but contains useful information for the students, for example, information about a class trip or a review of examination material for another school subject. The students thus have a reason for writing the passage.

4. The teacher asks a student to read out a corrected piece of his own writing for dictation.

5. The teacher dictates a poem that he wants the students to learn.

6. A useful variation is the dicto-comp. The teacher reads a passage all the way through, not broken into segments. Students listen to the passage two or three times. Then they pick up their pens and write down as close a version as possible. This makes them pay attention to the meaning of the passage more than to the form of individual words or the structure of the individual sentences. At the end of the passage, the students gather in small groups to compare what they have written down. After they have assembled everything they can remember, they listen to the passage again, make revisions and then check their grammar, spelling, and punctuation. They exchange papers with each other and remind each other of omitted points. Then the teacher either dictates again in segments, or writes up the complete version on the blackboard.

7. Checking a dictation immediately for accuracy of spelling and punctuation does not have to be the only way to end the activity. The teacher can collect the dictations, keep them and return them in a week. Then, in groups, students compare their versions and try to come up with one edited and corrected version that they all agree on. Once all the students in the class have before them a corrected accurate version of the dictated passage, they can then examine carefully the punctuation, grammar, and spelling. Such close reading can lead to the discovery of rules for, say, the use of the apostrophe, the spelling of **ie/ei**, or verb tenses in conditions. That same passage can then serve as the material for further controlled tasks, such as a controlled composition, with students changing present to past tense, or singular to plural subjects. Or the same passage can be presented a few weeks later with sentences scrambled or omitted; or students can summarize, continue, or respond to the passage.

NOTE-TAKING

In real life, when we need to listen and write, it is not always possible to write down every word we hear. People just do not talk at dictation speed. On the telephone, in the classroom, in everyday conversation, we write down a summary of what the speaker says, picking out the important information. The radio or the tape recorder is valuable here for providing additional material for students: dialogs to listen to, arguments to overhear, and speeches to react to. When elementary-level students take notes, they can be given a skeleton outline to work with and expand, so that their listening is more directed. Advanced students can listen to long passages and make notes as they listen. Both groups need to be alerted to the signals that speakers use: pauses, raising the head and the voice to make an important point, or using words like **first, finally, most important** to signal separation and priority of the points made.

Examples

1. Read aloud a passage that relates to a school subject or a current event. The students take notes. In groups, they compare the notes they have made. The teacher then distributes a copy of the original text or writes it on the board. The group decides on who wrote the best notes, and what makes those notes especially good.

2. The teacher reads a text aloud while students take notes. Then he distributes a copy of that text to one student in the

group, who reads it to the group again. Each student checks his notes and makes any necessary changes or additions. Then the students compare their versions and ask the student with the copy of the text to reread any parts they want to hear again. The group decides on one or two summaries that they will read aloud to the whole class.

3. The students go out on the street or watch an event together. They all take notes of what they observe. They write an account of what they saw from their notes. Then they read their accounts aloud and discuss the differences in their observations.

STORY-TELLING

Most people like stories. They like to hear them and often they like to tell them. When we hear or read a good story, we can't wait to find out what happens next. That is why detective novels and television serials are so popular. This natural curiosity to find out what happens in a story can be put to good use in a language classroom.

Examples

1. Read aloud a story—and this can also be used as a dictation—but stop at the point where the reader is likely to want to know how it continues. The students continue the story-writing. For example:

> One hot Tuesday in the middle of August, Sally didn't go to work. She wanted to be alone. She took a train to the seashore. She walked slowly along the beach until she was far away from the crowds, the ice cream sellers, and the lifeguards. Then she changed her clothes and ran into the cool water. She swam out a long way, enjoying the hot sun and the cool water. Then she saw . . .

The students read each other's continuations, and some read theirs aloud to the whole class. The teacher writes one, too, and reads it aloud. Or, the students in small groups listen to and then summarize each other's continuations. They read the summaries aloud to the whole class while the other students guess which student wrote each story. The last part of this activity is correction of what the students have written. They can be given specific guidelines for group work, such as, "Are all the verbs in the past tense? Are the verb forms correct? What is the best sentence? Which is the worst sentence? Can you do something about it?"

2. Give the students a list of words, such as **candle, house, steps, creak, scream, closet, potatoes,** and ask them to begin a story using those words. They must stop after a few minutes and pass their paper to another student, who will finish the story.

3. Play a game in class in which one student begins to tell a story, stops at an exciting point, and points to another student to continue the story. When most of the students have had a chance to participate, all the students then write down what they can remember of the story.

· ACTIVITIES ·

1. Find a writing task in a textbook. Discuss with other teachers how additional prewriting activities can be developed so that students speak, listen, and read as well as write.

2. Plan a sequence of activities for an elementary-level class so that your students would speak, listen, and read in preparation for writing about the two pictures on pp. 38–39. Write instructions for the students. Compare your activities with other teachers'.

3. Think back to a recent event that your students were interested in. Devise from the subject of this event a number of language activities that lead students to prepare for a writing assignment by using three of the techniques discussed in this chapter: brainstorming, guided discussion, and story-telling. Prepare a set of instructions for students.

4. Use the picture on page 47 to plan a guided discussion that will lead to a specific writing assignment. Write directions for the discussion and for the writing assignment.

5. Use the same picture on page 47 and write instructions for students to prepare a skit based on the picture. Then devise a writing task that either continues the action of the skit or reports on it. Write clear directions to the students for the writing task, including mention of the purpose and the audience for the piece of writing.

6. Find a reading passage that would be suitable for a dictation.

Explain how you would use it and why you would choose that particular dictation technique for that particular passage. What do you expect the students to learn from doing the dictation?

7. Imagine that you are using the reading passage on page 145 to read aloud so that students can take notes. Write the notes you hope they would write. Do you think the students might have difficulties with this? If so, where will the difficulties lie and what can you do to help?

·CHAPTER·SIX·
TECHNIQUES IN TEACHING PRACTICAL WRITING

There is no better way for students to grasp the essential value of writing as a form of communication than for them to produce the kind of practical writing that many people do in their everyday life. This practical writing has both a clear purpose and a specific audience. Much of this everyday writing is "writing to get things done."[1] Messages, forms, invitations, letters, and instructions are types of writing that anyone might have to do at some time or other. Often, in fact, one of the first things we have to do even on an airplane going into another country is fill out immigration and customs declaration forms. Upon arrival in the country, we might soon find it necessary to write a letter: a reply to an invitation, an apology, an inquiry, a complaint, a letter of thanks, congratulations, or sympathy. We might need to give directions on how to get from X to Y or give instructions on how to, for example, make a particular dish or perform a national dance. If our students experiment with these practical writing tasks in the classroom they will be not only practicing writing in the new language but also learning about the conventions of the new culture.

FORMS

It is useful to be able to fill out a form in another language. As a language classroom activity, too, the filling out of forms or questionnaires provides students with the opportunity to transfer information from one format to another. This manipulation of language—preserving the meaning while varying the form—allows for practice in forming and re-forming concepts in the new language.

Examples

1. Forms and interviews

If pairs of students interview each other as described in the last chapter, they can then transfer the information they receive onto a form. Role-playing can come into this, too, if the interviewer takes the part of interviewing an applicant for a job, filling out a form as the job interview proceeds. To involve the whole class in the activity, all the students can devise the form before the interviews begin, with the students deciding what information needs to be obtained and in what order.

Your students might also be given the task of interviewing someone they know—a friend, a colleague, a student in another class, for example—and completing a form for the purpose of completing a survey of people's family size, hobbies, or vacation preferences.

2. Forms and readings

From a short reading passage, students extract the necessary information to fill out a form:

> Beverly Amieva, a tall (5′8″), dark-haired woman, was born in 1953 in New Haven, Connecticut. She is married, with one daughter and one son. She works as a lawyer at the Legal Aid office in the business section of the city. She was educated at public schools in New Haven and at the University of Connecticut. She graduated from Columbia Law School in New York City in 1979.

The class can be organized in a variety of ways for an activity of this kind. Only one student of a pair has the passage, so that when he presents the information on a form, his partner has to reconstruct the description; or the students fill out a form as they listen to the passage above, then fill out a similar form for a person in their family. From this information another student constructs a descriptive paragraph.

3. Survey forms
In small groups, students discuss and draw up a questionnaire that aims at discovering attitudes other students might have towards controversial issues such as,

> a. It is best for your health to eat
>   2 ☐   3 ☐   4 ☐   meals a day.
> b. The most effective treatment for a bad cold is
>   food ☐   drinks ☐   rest ☐   medicine ☐.

Students from one group then move around the room to interview students in another group to gather information for the questionnaire. When they have collected a few responses, they organize the information they have received and present it to the class either in a narrative or in statistical form, such as in a graph or a table.

LETTERS

If a language student will ever need to write anything in the second language, it will probably be a letter. Letters are one of the most widespread forms of written communication. For this reason, we have to devote classroom time to teaching letter writing. But it is not only because letters are so useful that we should do this. Teaching letter writing also gives us the chance to deal with a variety of forms and functions that are an essential part of language mastery. We write letters to invite, explain, apologize, commiserate, congratulate, complain, inquire, order, apply, acknowledge, and thank. Each of these language functions has its own associated vocabulary, connotations, sentence structures, and appropriate choice of words and tone to fit the audience. Within each function there are various levels of formality and informality. Letter-writing tasks make students consider their audience as well as their accuracy.

Examples

1. Letters and forms

Present a situation to the class, such as looking for a job through a summer job employment agency. Various jobs are advertised there—office clerk, salesperson in a bookstore, supermarket cashier, gas station attendant, babysitter, and farm worker. Show the class a sample advertisement for a job and discuss it:

WANTED

Salesperson for June–August in busy bookstore. Hours 9–6, Mon–Sat. Some heavy lifting. Prev. exp. and good health essential. Apply: The Manager, Catskill Bookstore, Water Street, Catskill.

Then explain the form and mechanics of writing a letter of application for a job. Deal with the addresses, date, greeting, closing, punctuation, and spacing. Show the class a sample of a letter of application, such as the one below:

> 259 Hill Street
> Catskill, NY 12414
> June 5, 1984

The Manager
Catskill Bookstore
Water Street
Catskill, NY 12414

Dear Sir:

I would like to apply for the job of summer salesperson, which you advertised in today's *Daily Mail.* I have just graduated from Catskill High School with good grades in English and History. I was editor of the school newspaper. I read a lot in my spare time and last summer I even worked in the Main Street bookstore in my grandparents' home town of Putney, Vermont. I was born in Putney on October 22, 1964, and I have been living at the above address for twelve years.

I am 5′8″ tall and weigh 145 lbs. I was a member

of my school swim team, so I am very strong and healthy.

If you require a letter of reference about my work and ability, please write to Ms. Nancy Adams, the manager of the Main Street bookstore in Putney.

Yours truly,

Deborah Johnson

Deborah Johnson

Now give each pair of students an advertisement for a job. One of the pair writes his own letter of application for the advertised job, while the other fills out a registration form like this one:

Catskill Summer Employment Agency
Registration Form

Name _____ _____ _____
                 First   Middle   Last

Address _____

Date of birth _____ Birthplace _____
               Month/Day/Year

Height _____ Weight _____ Health _____

Schools attended _____

_____

Previous work experience _____

Hobbies _____

References _____

The students then exchange their forms and letters. Using the information in the registration form he now has, one student writes a letter of application, pretending that he is his partner. Similarly, the other student, who now has a letter in front of him, fills out a registration form using the information given in the letter his partner wrote.[2]

2. Informal letters

Establish a situation in the classroom; for example, the students are to invite another student to a party, or students are to ask each other questions. The students then write informal notes to each other. A mailbox in the classroom could make this activity a daily one in your ESL classroom. Students can be encouraged to make real requests and ask real questions: "Do you have any picture postcards from your friends in New York? Will you bring them to class tomorrow?" They can also write a note to the teacher, for example, "Will you please explain what *informal* means? Sincerely, Tamal."

Textbook characters can be made more alive if students are encouraged to assume the characters' roles and correspond with each other in those roles. In this way, they can continue the material of the dialogs and stories in the textbook.

3. Business letters

Once students know the form of a business letter, they can be given communicative writing tasks that lead to them to practice this useful form. The writing of business letters in the classroom can be tied in very neatly with lessons on the functions of language (how to apologize, complain, inquire, for example, and the pertinent vocabulary and expressions to use for these functions). Letter writing can also very often be the outcome of a skit or a role-playing scene; still in the role that was adopted for discussion, the student writes a business letter. The recipient of the letter will then actually be in the classroom, also acting in a role. Students who have real requests or complaints to make can of course be encouraged to write real letters and then actually to mail them. That is certainly a situation in which students will check their grammar and spelling very carefully without even being told to by the teacher.

Models and parallel writings are of use, too, when dealing with business letters. The letter of application for a job on page 86, for instance, could serve a student as a model when he has to write a letter of application for a job as an office clerk. The information to be included in the letter can be given to the student on a form, such as the one on page 87. The student then uses that information to write a letter similar to the model.

4. Pen pals

When students have pen pals from another country, they feel the need to communicate clearly. If a teacher can arrange for a whole class of students to correspond with a class in another country, then letter writing can become a regular feature of the class. What is more, these classroom writings can then actually be mailed and the students will receive an answer. Setting this up takes time, but it is not difficult. Teachers from other countries wishing to find whole classes of English-speaking pen pals can write to the presidents of local affiliate organizations of the International TESOL organization for information. (Information about local organizations affiliated to TESOL (Teachers of English to Speakers of Other Languages) can be obtained from: TESOL, School of Languages and Linguistics, Georgetown University, Washington, D.C., U.S.A.)

LISTS

Lists are a much neglected part of writing in a second language, even though a lot of the writing that people do is list making. People write lists to help them remember what to do. They write shopping lists, lists of people to invite to a party, and lists of things to do tomorrow. Lists are the basis for many conceptual activities; with a list before them, people alphabetize, group, and classify. As the system of classification into categories may vary from culture to culture, it is important for students studying a second language to be aware of the classification systems of that language.

Examples

1. Students begin by brainstorming and writing down what they would take with them for a week of hiking in the mountains. A typical list of words produced might be:

shorts	sleeping bag	matches	knife
sweater	tent	cooking pot	flashlight
bathing suit	mosquito net	boots	

Then they alphabetize the items (one method of dealing with a list!) and decide which categories they can sort the words into: clothing, cooking items, daily necessities, etc. This kind of classifying of information is an important first step in the organization of a piece of writing. Students see that they have to reject some information if it does not fit one chosen category, or they might need to provide more information to fill out another category. They also see very clearly how they might go about organizing a piece of writing called "Advice to a Hiker in the Mountains."

2. An everyday task of making a shopping list can be developed into an activity that is useful for writing a composition. Ask all the students, quite simply, what they have to buy in the next day or so and write a list on the board. If one person were going to buy all those things, you ask, would he just begin at the top of the list and work his way down? No, he would group the items— all the food together, the clothes, the toiletries, the household items. This kind of task can be followed with a conceptually similar task of grouping ideas about a topic, ideas that are no longer in single words but in sentences. Students will see that the same principle of looking, seeing similarities, and grouping is useful in both cases.

DAILY NOTES

Just as many people write lists but do not show them to anyone else, so many people also keep daily notebooks or journals. They write a record of the events of the day or their ideas about those events. The fact that this is personal writing does not exclude it from classroom use. When people write every day, for their own eyes and not to be judged by another, they often find that they can write more and more each day. Their fluency increases. They labor less over each word. When they write about something that concerns them, they worry less about being "correct." All of this is useful in learning to write.

Examples

1. Ask students to keep a special notebook and to write in it in English for a few minutes every day: a reaction to something they saw or read, an account of an event, or a description of a feeling. You can check periodically to see that the students are in fact doing it, but it is better if this personal writing remains ungraded. Occasionally, ask students to read back over their writing and to select something they wrote about that they would like to develop into a composition. Or ask students to volunteer to read some sections to the class so that the other students can respond.

2. Allow a few minutes at the end of each class for students to write in their notebooks a summary of what happened in the class. From what they write, you can often discover quite a lot about your own lessons!

3. Begin some classes by letting students write for ten minutes on any topic. They write as much and as quickly as they can. If they can't think of a word in English, they just write it in their native language. It is good to encourage some students to volunteer to read aloud what they have written, for then the lesson begins with an emphasis on writing for communication of ideas.

INSTRUCTIONS

We write to tell friends how to find our house, we write instructions for a neighbor on how to water our plants, feed our canary, or walk our dog, we write a recipe for a friend, we write to an absent child with advice on how to avoid being homesick. Writing instructions is such a common writing activity that language learners need to learn how to do it. There is a variety of classroom techniques that have developed around this activity. Just as writing daily notes taps the student's inner thoughts, likes, and dislikes, the writing of real instructions taps the student's skills. What is he good at? What can he tell others how to do? Ski, make a table, ride a motorcycle, change a flat tire, make a boomerang, do a magic card trick, bake a cake, ride a horse, perform a dance. . .? The list is endless.

Examples
1. Ask students to interview each other to find out what the other person knows how to do. The interviewer takes notes on the steps

in the procedure, and then tries to write the instructions. At some point in the process of the note-taking and the writing, show the students a passage that gives instructions and uses signal words like **first, second, next, then,** and **finally**.

2. Students write instructions for each other as to how to get from the school to their home. The readers ask questions if they need to.

3. Instructions form the basis for a rather noisy but often successful game: a treasure hunt. Groups of students are given an object which they hide somewhere in the building. Then they write directions for another group to find the object, with the instructions written as if the reader did not know the building at all. Then, of course, the groups try to follow the directions.

· ACTIVITIES ·

1. Write some daily notes in your second language; write for at least ten minutes a day every day for a few weeks. Then discuss with other teachers what you wrote about, how you felt about writing it, and what (if any) difficulties you experienced.

2. Make a list of where you might be able to get the following for classroom use:
a. English-language newspapers with job and housing advertisements in them;
b. business or travel brochures in English;
c. sets of instructions in English;
d. application forms in English.
Explore, for example, consulates, embassies, factories, businesses, travel agencies, and libraries. Share your list with other teachers and discuss how these resources could be useful to you in your writing class.

3. What practical writing activities can you devise for a lesson based on the picture on page 124? In what ways can the student work with (a) forms, (b) letters, (c) lists, and (d) instructions? Write directions for students for each of these tasks.

4. Write instructions for students to write a letter from the Catskill Bookstore Manager to Debbie Johnson in reply to the letter on pp. 86-87. Give them some guidance on the type of information they should include.

5. Prepare a classroom activity in which students can write informal letters to each other and exchange real information.

6. Find an example of a letter in a textbook or write one your-self. Using this letter as a model, prepare a group writing activity that lets the students in the class write letters and answer them.

·CHAPTER SEVEN·

TECHNIQUES IN USING CONTROLLED WRITING

Throughout this book, you will find suggestions for controlled writing tasks. My definition of controlled writing is all the writing your students do for which a great deal of the content and/or form is supplied. It is the opposite of free writing, where students generate, organize, and express their own ideas, in their own sentences. In controlled tasks, more is given to the students: an outline to complete, a paragraph to manipulate, a model to follow, or a passage to continue, for example.

Controlled writing is a useful tool at all levels of composition teaching and not just in the early stages before students have gained enough fluency to handle free writing. Of course, it is with that word *enough* that the difficulty arises. How much language acquisition is enough for a student to be able to write a few sentences? We let students speak their new language as much as possible, we give them exercises for practice, we encourage them to try to express themselves, and we are delighted if we understand what they say. We give them help as they go along, correcting grammar, supplying an idiom, suggesting a word. In writing, too, they need the same opportunity to get words down on paper as soon as possible and to try out the written language. Only then will they acquire enough familiarity with writing to be able to approach more challenging tasks with confidence.

Controlled writing tasks give students focused practice in getting words down on paper and in concentrating on one or two problems at a time; they are thus spared from tackling the full range of complexity that free writing entails. For the teacher, controlled writing is easier to mark and much less time-consuming, so more can be assigned. If the student is steered away from choosing content or what to say about a topic because it is supplied, then both the student and the teacher can devote full attention to mastery of the focal point of the controlled writing, whether that is the use of past tense endings or the tenses used in indirect speech.

Controlled writing can fit into a composition curriculum at any level of student ability in these two places:

1. before free writing, when students practice a grammatical point or syntactic structure within a text and not just as a sentence exercise, and, at the same time, use that text as a source of vocabulary, ideas, idioms, and organization to help them in planning their own piece of writing;

2. after free writing, when we see what problems our students are having and assign a controlled task to give them practice with the problem areas.

The fact that students are performing the same operations on a common text makes controlled tasks highly suitable for small-group or whole-class discussion. Students can work together on deciding on one "right answer" or on a possible range of options for the answer for each of the tasks within the controlled writing. So even though the students are not communicating real information to each other or to any reader in their writing, they are in their discussion communicating with each other about how best to complete the task.

I have divided controlled writing into five different types of frequently assigned tasks. None of these in any way constitutes a total composition program. Each, however, has value in any program when both teacher and students know clearly what the tasks are designed to accomplish. They are not just general "writing practice"; their greatest value comes from the fact that they provide practice in a specific feature of the written language or the process of writing. Teachers should assign these five types of controlled writing—controlled composition, question and

answer, guided composition, parallel writing, and sentence combining—with their focus and purpose in mind: not "I think I'll
assign a controlled composition today," but "My students need
practice with (subject-verb agreement, adjective phrases, synonyms, etc.) so I'll assign a controlled composition for them to
discuss in class."

CONTROLLED COMPOSITION

When students write a controlled composition exercise, they are
given a passage to work with; they do not, therefore, have to concern themselves with content, organization, finding ideas, and
forming sentences. They write the given passage down, making
a few specified changes, usually of a grammatical or structural
nature. They might, for example, rewrite a passage describing **a
man** to tell the reader about **two men,** making only the necessary
singular/plural changes. Or they will rewrite a present tense passage in the past, or a passage of direct speech in indirect speech.
Sometimes they will be directed to change only three designated
sentences from active to passive, or to convert relative clauses to
post-nominal modifiers (the woman who is waiting at the bus
stop / the woman waiting at the bus stop). They will, that is, make
changes in the passage that was given to them, but they will not
add anything of their own to it. There are "right answers," so it
is possible for students to produce a composition that is 100 percent accurate.

Controlled composition focuses the students' attention on
specific features of the written language. It is a good method of
reinforcing grammar, vocabulary, and syntax in context. In addition, as the students write the passages, they are using the conventions of written English, such as indentation, punctuation,
connecting words, and spelling. Most of the controlled composition textbooks available set up the tasks so that the book can be
used for individualized instruction, with students proceeding at
their own pace.[1] (One word of warning is necessary here: Before
assigning a controlled composition, do it yourself to make sure
that the student's finished product will be real English. A passage
of all negative sentences, all passive verb forms, or all parallel

structures is just not normal written English.) The examples that
follow indicate the variety of materials and tasks that controlled
composition offers.

Examples

1. Students work in small groups to agree on each change in this
passage:

> You are a police detective who has been follow-
> ing a man every day for a month. You write this report
> for your supervisor:

> "Every day, C.P. gets up at 7 a.m. He walks to a
> local store to buy a newspaper. He reads the obituaries.
> Then he makes three different telephone calls from
> three different public pay phones. He goes to a coffee
> shop and waits outside. A tall blond woman driving a
> silver Cadillac picks him up."

> Your supervisor then tells you that she wants a
> specific report on what C.P. did on Wednesday last
> week. Change the report. Begin with "Last Wednes-
> day, C.P. got up at 7 a.m."

Notice that in doing this exercise, the students cannot automatically change every verb they see; they have to be alert and decide
that **buy** and **driving** remain the same. Notice, too, how easy it
is for the teacher to mark the finished piece of writing, particularly if the students underline every change they make.

2. In some controlled compositions, the making of one change
necessitates other linguistic changes. The student has to be
aware of these and has to make the necessary connections. The
following is a controlled composition task from a textbook for
beginning and intermediate students:[2]

> [1]It's morning in the park. [2]A young man is walk-
> ing with his dog. [3]Every day he buys a newspaper at
> the newsstand. [4]The news dealer greets him. [5]The man
> takes his newspaper to a nearby bench. [6]He sits by

himself and reads. [7]His dog runs in the trees.

Rewrite the passage, but change **A young man** to **Two young men** in sentence 2.([2])

Students have to be alert to much more than simply changing **man** to **men** throughout. They have to deal with:
a. verb forms: **is-are; buys-buy; takes-take; sits-sit; reads-read; runs-run** (but **greets** remains unchanged);
b. noun plurals: **man-men; newspaper-newspapers; dog-dogs;**
c. pronouns: **he-they; him-them;**
d. possessive adjectives: **his-their;**
e. reflexive pronouns: **himself-themselves;**
f. determiners: **a newspaper-newspapers.**

And while they are writing the completed paragraph, they have to pay attention to indentation, capitalization, punctuation, and spelling. So even though the task is controlled, the students still have to do a lot of thinking.

3. Some controlled composition tasks ask students to fill in vocabulary words in a passage; the advantage of this over single-sentence exercises is that the coherence that the text demands must influence the choice of words throughout the text as in the following example:

I went to a (1) to buy (2) presents for my (3). I have two (4), William and Walter, and two (5), Joyce and Joan. There were a lot of (6) on the shelves and I began by choosing (7) for both the boys. I know that both of them like (8). The girls are younger. After looking at several (9) I finally bought them both (10).

(1) bookshop, toyshop
(2) birthday, Christmas
(3) nephews and nieces, grandchildren
(4) grandsons, nephews
(5) nieces, granddaughters
(6) children's books, toys
(7) books, model cars

(8) automobiles, adventure stories

(9) picture books, toys for girls

(10) dolls, books of nursery rhymes[3]

4. A controlled composition can provide a structural skeleton outline so that students can construct a parallel paragraph using new information:

Sheila and Maura are sisters. They would like to wear each other's clothes, but they can't. They wear different sizes. Look at their sizes:

	Sheila	**Maura**
Dress size	10	14
Shoe size	7	8
Blouse size	34	38
Glove size	7	7
Belt size	26	28

Now, look at this paragraph that Sheila wrote:

(1) My dresses are too small for Maura to wear. (2) My shoes are not big enough for her, either. (3) My blouses are also too small for her to wear. (4) However, I wear the same size gloves as she does. (5) I like to wear belts, but, unfortunately, Maura's belts are too large for me.

Rewrite the paragraph from Maura's point of view. Fill in the blanks below:

(1) My dresses are _____ _____ _____ Sheila _____ wear. (2) My shoes are too _____ _____ her, too. (3) My blouses are also _____ _____ _____ her _____ wear. (4) However, I wear _____ _____ _____ gloves _____ she does. (5) I like to wear belts, but, unfortunately, Sheila's belts are not _____ _____ _____ me.

Look at the paragraph about Sheila. Write a similar paragraph about Winston and Anthony, who are brothers. Rewrite the information from Winston's point of view. Use the information below:

	Winston	**Anthony**
Coat size	36	38
Trouser size	30	32
Shirt size	15	15½
Shoe size	10	10
Hat size	7	7⅛

Your first sentence:
My coats are too small for Anthony to wear.[4]

5. Controlled compositions can also address the problems of advanced-level students: they can be asked to supply synonyms for specific words, to change post-nominal adjectival phrases into adjectives (a life of sobriety/ a sober life), or to change the focus of a passage by switching it from positive to negative or vice-versa (a passage about an optimist becomes a passage about a pessimist, for example).

Material for controlled compositions is available not only in specialized textbooks, but also in the short reading passages found in most ESL texts, and of course in the writing of the students themselves. A student's composition, once revised and corrected for grammar, can then be used by that same student or by the whole class as a text to change.

QUESTION AND ANSWER

The type of controlled composition that uses a question and answer format allows students a little more freedom in structuring sentences. They are not given the actual text that they will write; rather, they are given a series of questions, the answers to which form the text. Carefully constructed questions will produce a coherent text.

Examples
1. Questions can ask about information which is given in notes or a list or even in a picture sequence. The following list shows an army recruit's daily routine:

6:00 get up
6:05 make bed
6:10 polish boots and buttons
6:20 put on uniform
6:25 march to the mess hall
6:30 eat breakfast
6:45 do exercises

The students write a paragraph that describes the daily routine of Billy, a new recruit, by answering the following questions in complete sentences:

- When does Billy get up?
- What does he do first?
- What does he do next?
- What does he do then?
- When does he march to the mess hall?
- What does he do there?
- What does he do after breakfast?
- Is the beginning of his day leisurely or very busy?

If the students are able to, they could also combine some of the sentences.

2. Questions can also serve to draw forth and structure the students' own responses. They can elicit personal information (**In what year were you born? Where have you lived for most of your life?** etc.) or depend upon a vivid imagination (**In what month did Sunnyville get its biggest snowstorm ever? How deep were the snow drifts? What things did the snow bury?** etc.).Question-and-answer compositions based on personal information are useful at the beginning of a school year or semester, when teachers and students need to learn about each other. For the teacher, any information about students' likes, dislikes, interests, and hobbies is useful for devising future topics for discussion and writing.

3. A question-and-answer composition is a good follow-up exercise to a reading passage. Students read or listen to a passage two or three times. Then, without further reference to the passage, they write a composition based on a given set of questions about the material they have just studied. Such tasks provide an excellent opportunity for teachers to tie language study in with the study of other school subjects.

GUIDED COMPOSITION

Guided composition is an extension of controlled composition. It is less controlled than the above examples of controlled composition in that it gives students some but not all of the content and form of the sentences they will use. Their finished products will thus be similar but not exactly alike. Students are given a first sentence, a last sentence, an outline to fill out, a series of questions to respond to, or information to include in their piece of writing. As with any free writing task, with guided composition, too, students should be able to discuss, make notes, share findings, and plan strategies together before they begin to write.

Examples
1. Students look at and discuss the picture (on page 104), and any new vocabulary words or idioms are written on the board. Then the students are given these guidelines for writing:

Write three paragraphs about Grant Wood's painting *American Gothic.*

a. Begin by telling your reader that the picture shows a couple standing in front of a house. Then describe the house: tell your reader if it is in the city or the country, what color it is, what it is made of, what shape the windows are; tell your reader, too, if the house looks inviting or uninviting. If it reminds you of any other type of building, mention that also.

b. Start your second paragraph by saying something about the woman: Is she, for example, young, old, pretty, stern-looking, fashionable, simply dressed? Then write a sentence each about her hair, her facial expression, and her clothes.

c. Begin your last paragraph with "Standing next to the woman is a man." Go on to tell your reader if you think he is her husband, and why or why not. Then write a sentence each about his

Grant Wood, *American Gothic,* Collection of The Art
Institute of Chicago. Reprinted by permission.

features, his glasses, his expression, his clothes, and the tool he is holding (a pitchfork).

Now discuss with your classmates and your teacher what two or three sentences you could write to finish off the piece of writing.[5]

2. The same picture, *American Gothic,* can provide much looser guidelines for a guided composition. Students could, for instance, be asked simply to write three paragraphs about the picture, one describing the setting, one the woman, and one the man. Or they could be given the first sentence of each paragraph. All of these sample assignments can, of course, be discussed by students beforehand and students can even work in pairs to produce one piece of writing with two names on it. For all these tasks, students will need to use the present tense, possessives, and expressions with **look** (**she looks strict; it looks like a church,** etc.), so these can be reviewed during discussion.

3. Guided composition topics can also be directed towards the students' own experience or observation. If an opening sentence is given to the whole class, then the details they use to explain and illustrate it can be compared. Some compositions can be read aloud or written on the board so that students can see how others in their class tackled the same task:

> Write a paragraph beginning with: "The way we view time in [name of country] has certain distinctive features." (Include details on how long a school day or work day is, how long people take for lunch, when people eat their evening meal, how long it is before someone is considered to be "late" for an appointment, etc.)

4. A simple outline can be the basis for in-class discussion which then leads to writing:

> Discuss the degree of freedom permitted the young people of today in a country you know well:
> a. How the subject of marriage is initiated
> b. Preliminary steps

c. Possible financial arrangements
d. Opportunity for choice of mate
e. Opportunity to become acquainted with mate decided upon
f. Your comment[6]

5. Giving students the first and last sentence of a paragraph controls very strictly the content and many of the grammatical features the students will use, yet the students are free to compose their own sentences, as in this task:

> Use your imagination and compose four or five sentences to complete the paragraph:
> • My sister bought a lottery ticket.
> • If she had not lost her handbag, she would have won a big prize.[7]

6. Notice how the following task leads students to use words of contrast:

> Complete the paragraph with the information given:
> • Although Lincoln and Stephen are twins, they are very different.
>
> | **Lincoln** | **Stephen** |
> | --- | --- |
> | tall | short |
> | dark | fair |
> | studious | sporty |
> | a lawyer | a jazz musician |

Here students can either be expected to provide the connecting words themselves, or they can be given more explicit guidance:

> Write four more sentences about Lincoln and Stephen, using the information in the lists. In addition, use the following words:
> Sentence 1: First, _____, but
> Sentence 2: Second, _____ while
> Sentence 3: Third, _____;
> Sentence 4: Finally, _____; Stephen, on the other hand,

7. A picture sequence provides excellent material for a guided composition. The pictures provide the subject matter, and class discussion will provide vocabulary and grammatical features needed to write about the sequence. If half of the class is given one set of pictures and the other half another, then the task can be simply to describe the events to each other. Or the last picture of the sequence can be omitted, and students then finish the story by using their imagination. The section on "Picture Sets" in Chapter 3 provides examples.

SENTENCE COMBINING

Sentence combining is the combining of "base" or "kernel" sentences into one longer compound or complex sentence. As a technique to help students with their writing, it has been of interest to teachers for the last ten years. Researchers on writing for native speakers have found that sentence-combining exercises improve students' sentence structure, length of sentence, and sentence variety.[8] For ESL students, sentence combining is certainly a very good way of introducing new language structures without going into complicated explanations and employing specialized terminology. While it does not give students the opportunity to formulate ideas and communicate something meaningful to a reader, it does provide plenty of practice with the syntactic structures that are more common in writing than in speech, and gives students the chance to use the grammatical knowledge they have to make choices about structure.[9]

The student who is asked to combine sentences is given his content. His decision is not one of *what* to say but of *how* to say it. Various degrees of control determine the amount of freedom the writer exercises in choosing which structure to use.

Examples
1. Students are given pairs of simple sentences, taken from a textbook paragraph or from the students' own writing, to combine into one sentence within the context of the paragraph. This activity is suitable for small groups as students can pool their

resources and between them discover as many options as possible. In these two sentences:

- She didn't see the beginning of the play.
- The train was late.

the students could discover these possibilities for combination:

- Since/As/Because the train was late, she . . .
- She didn't see the beginning of the movie because (as/since) the train was late.
- The train was late, so she . . .
- With the train being so late, she . . .

Then they choose which version fits best into the larger context of the paragraph. With an elementary-level class, you can supply a cue:

- She didn't see the beginning of the play.
- The train was late.   (because)

The students then have to decide where to use the joining word, how to arrange the sentences around it, and how to punctuate the new sentence.

2. Sentence-combining tasks are not restricted to improving a text. The teacher can concentrate on the production of a new text by asking students to combine groups of sentences so that the finished series of sentences makes up a paragraph:

    a.   1. It is early morning.
          2. Gus is driving to work.

    b.   1. He sees a hitchhiker.
          2. The hitchhiker is by the road.
          3. He stops his car.
          4. He stops to give the hitchhiker a ride.
             —and so on.[10]

Student involvement and comprehension of the whole story can also be increased if one student is asked to supply the final group of sentences for other students in the class to combine.

3. At high intermediate and advanced levels, students can be given a reading passage containing complex sentences which they then break down into kernel sentences for other students to combine. This provides excellent practice in analyzing sentence structure and discovering how sentences are assembled in English.

PARALLEL WRITING

Parallel writing is, in a way, the freest kind of controlled writing. Instead of making changes in a given passage or writing according to an outline or given sentences, students read and study a passage and then write their own on a similar theme, using as a guide the vocabulary, sentence structure, cohesive devices, and organization of the model passage. The use of parallel pictures for guided parallel writing practice was described in Chapter 3. Readings, dictations, tapes, and textbook dialogs can also be used.

Examples
1. The students read or listen to a textbook dialog a few times. Then they write down what they heard or read, though now not in dialog form but as a narrative. So this:

> Sue: I'm leaving.

becomes: Sue said firmly that she was leaving (she was going to leave/was about to leave/intended to leave).

2. The students listen to a series of short descriptions of people. In front of them they have a table with some information missing, which they have to fill in from the information given in the description:[11]

Name	Age	Hair	Height	Clothes
Ann Marie		long, black		
Rosa	17		quite tall	a gray skirt and a blue sweater

Then they write a description of each person, using the given and the collected information.

Now that the students have practiced describing a person using given information, they use what they have written as a guide to writing a description of another student in the class, without giving the student's name. The following height chart might be useful:[12]

HEIGHT		MEN	WOMEN
6'0"	1.85	tall	very tall
5'10"	1.80	quite tall	tall
5'6"	1.70	quite short	quite tall
5'3"	1.60	short	quite short
5'0"	1.50	very short	short
4'10"	1.45	very short	very short

Each student reads his description aloud and the class guesses who is being described.

3. Letters, dialogs, and stories lend themselves well to parallel writing exercises. After reading, the students are given an outline of a different set of information and write a passage that is parallel to the one they have just read. An example of this can be done with the following:

Dear Ms. Johnson:

Thank you for your letter applying for a job as a waitress at Waterside Camp. It is important for you to know what your duties will be. First, you will have to set the tables. Second, you will have to carry the food from the kitchen to the table and serve it to the campers. Third, you will have to clear the tables and take the dishes back to the kitchen. Finally, you should know that we serve breakfast at 7 a.m., so you'll have to be on duty every day at 6 a.m.

Please let me know if you would like to arrange an interview.

Sincerely yours,

Karen Greene

Karen Greene

Debbie Johnson decided not to work at the camp. Instead, she applied for a job in a bookstore (see her letter on pp. 86-87). Write a letter from the manager of the bookstore, Helen Rogers, to Debbie Johnson, telling her about the job. You can use the following ideas and others of your own in your letter:
• check the orders
• keep a record of all the books sold
• put the books on the shelves
• keep the books clean and neat on the shelves
• serve food at the bookstore's Saturday evening parties for authors (until 9 p.m.)[13]

4. Parallel writing assignments can vary in the amount of control or guidance the student is offered. A tightly controlled exercise asks a student to read a short passage and then rewrite it with different but given subject matter:

Read this description of the port of Calcutta and then write a similar description of New York. The necessary information is given below:

Calcutta is a port in India. It is situated on the northeast coast, on the estuary of the River Hooghly, which flows into the Bay of Bengal. The population of the City is six million. The distance from New Delhi, the capital of the country, is about one thousand miles.

New York—the U.S.A.—east coast—River Hudson—Atlantic Ocean—eight million—Washington—two hundred and fifty miles.[14]

5. Far more freedom to use the imagination is given in the type of parallel writing exercise that asks students to write about an event from the point of view of another person. The following is such an exercise:

Read this passage carefully.

Jim arrived home and discovered that he had forgotten his door key. He rang the bell, but nobody came to open the door. He rang again, and waited, but still there was no answer. He walked round the house to see if he could find an open window, but they were all locked. It was beginning to rain and he didn't know what to do. Dorothy, his wife, had obviously gone out, and he didn't know where she had gone to, or when she would return. He waited for half an hour. Still nobody came. Finally, feeling wet and cold and angry, he picked up a big stone and threw it through the kitchen window. Just as he had unlocked the window and was climbing through it he heard the front door open. His wife had come back!

Relate this incident as it might be told by Dorothy. Begin like this: Jim, my husband, always arrives home from work at 6 p.m. One evening I had to go out unexpectedly, . . .[15]

Here students invent their own sentences, but they follow the story outline that the model provides, and use the past tense and much of the given vocabulary. This writing from a new viewpoint can be extended to parallel writing using a passage from literature as a model. One such exercise is to read a passage from James Joyce's *Dubliners* that describes all the food on the supper table at an Irish party; the student then has to describe a table set with his own national dishes.[16]

· ACTIVITIES ·

1. Find a short reading passage in English that is suitable for the level of the class you teach. Use this passage to devise:
a. a controlled composition
b. a question-and-answer controlled composition
c. a guided composition

2. Imagine that the students in your class are having problems using the conditional structure: "If you learn these words, you will pass the test." Devise a parallel writing task that will allow the students to practice using this structure. You may either find a model passage or write one of your own.

3. Write a paragraph describing a recent event. Take the paragraph and make up a sentence-combining exercise from it. What structures will your exercise provide practice with?

4. Adapt the following passage to give students practice in (a) sentence combining, (b) parallel writing, and (c) controlled composition focusing on verb tense. Write instructions for the students for each of those tasks.

> The telephone rang three times. Helen got up from the armchair slowly. She put her book down, stretched, and yawned. Then she sauntered over to the phone. She was deliberately slow. It made me angry to watch her. Still yawning, she picked up the phone and listened. I saw her face change. The silence was broken by a shriek and a crash as she dropped the phone and ran out of the room.

5. Using the reading passage on pp. 111-12 beginning with "Jim arrived home ... ," write instructions for students for a controlled composition task that will give them practice with the personal pronouns **he** and **she** and the possessive adjectives **his** and **her.** Remember to specify a purpose for the piece of writing.

6. Use the same passage on pp. 111-12 and prepare from it a sentence-combining task for your students. Rewrite some of the compound and complex sentences as base sentences, such as:

> He rang the bell.
> Nobody came to open the door.

Write instructions for students to combine the sentences. Decide whether or not to provide cues.

7. Use the letter on page 110 to prepare the guidelines for a guided composition.

·CHAPTER EIGHT·
TECHNIQUES IN TEACHING ORGANIZATION

While controlled writing tasks give students the opportunity to produce a great deal of almost error-free writing and also to focus their attention on troublesome grammatical and syntactic features, they provide only reinforcement and not a total writing program. As soon as your students develop their writing skills enough to be writing their own sentences instead of just following a pattern or transforming given sentences, then they are ready to write a sequence of sentences. This sequence comprises free writing. When students write even only a few sentences of their own, they are suddenly responsible for all the things that are usually provided for them in a controlled task. Now they have to think about what to write about, which words and sentences to choose, and how to organize the ideas.

The organization of written discourse in English is culturally determined in the same way as are eating habits and social interaction. How we write in English has as many conventions as how we use a knife and fork. (Both eating and writing show differences between British and American conventions!) So students who write well in their first language cannot simply rely on an accurate translation of their sentences into English. There is a decidedly "English" way of handling a topic, of putting the sentences together, and of connecting the sentences. What works as a piece of writing in one language does not always work in another, however skillful the translation. Students in our classes have to learn not only how English sentences are formed but how paragraphs and longer pieces are constructed. If the writer addresses all the writer's concerns in the diagram on page 6 but pays no attention to the way ideas are organized, the result can be a very un-English text.

In written English, we state our topic (our main idea, focus, point of view), and we usually elaborate on our statement by adding supporting details, such as facts, examples, descriptions, illustrations, reasons, causes, effects, comparisons, and contrasts. In short, we show our reader that there is a basis for the statement we made. Our reader's expectations, our own purpose, and our content lead us to choose the way we will present our ideas. Organization, that is, does not occur to us first. Ideas do.

Organizing your thoughts in writing is, like writing itself, a process. It's a process of moving back and forth from general statements to specific details, of finding appropriate and relevant details and arranging them in the most effective order. It's also a process of moving back and forth between reading and writing: writing something down, reading it over, searching for more material by discussion or reading, reading to discover how other writers organize their meaning, and then writing again.

The techniques that follow therefore involve both reading and writing. They allow students to perceive the choices a writer has before him to meet the reader's needs and to make choices with the writer's purpose and meaning firmly in mind.

OUTLINES

There are two basic types of outlines:

1. an outline the writer makes before writing the text;
2. an outline the writer makes of what he has already written.

Both are useful. An outline that is developed before writing should be brief and should be made only after extensive discussion, reading, list-making, brainstorming, and other prewriting activities. It should, that is, be a device to guide the writer and not something to lock him into a cage that he couldn't escape from if he wanted to! An outline that is made after a text has been produced, that is, after the first draft, helps the writer see clearly what he has done and what he needs to do to make his meaning clearer to the reader. It also points to new directions the piece of writing might take.

Analysis of pieces of writing by professional writers (or textbook writers) is helpful. Frequently students can see clarity of organization even in a very difficult piece, and seeing the pattern helps them understand the piece and appreciate the value of a clear organizational scheme.

Examples

1. Give the students a reading passage such as the one below. Ask them either to discuss and make their own outline of what has been written or to complete the skeleton of a given outline:

Owning a Car

Should a person own a car? This is an important question. In a large urban area, there are some good reasons for owning a car. First, a car allows a person to move around freely. With a car, there is no need to check a bus schedule or wait for a train. Second, a car is a comfortable way to travel, especially in the wintertime. In bad weather, the driver stays warm and dry, while the poor bus or train rider might have to stand in the rain. Finally, a driver is usually safe in a car at night. The rider might need to walk down a dark street to get to a stop, or wait on a dark corner.

There are, on the other hand, many good reasons against owning a car. First, it can be very expensive. The price of fuel continues to rise and car insurance can cost three or four hundred dollars a year. In addition, it is expensive to maintain and repair a car. A simple tune-up can cost $50. In an urban area, it might also be expensive to park the car. Second, owning a car can cause worry and stress. It is exhausting to drive in rush-hour traffic, or to drive around and around looking for a parking space. If you leave your car on the street, it might get stolen. That is something else to worry about. Finally, everyone needs to think about

pollution and energy problems. Air pollution and
noise pollution increase as more and more people
drive cars. More and more cars also burn more and
more fuel. At present, drivers may have to wait in long
lines at filling stations in order to buy a couple of gal-
lons of gasoline.

Should a person in an urban area own a car? In
order to answer the question, a person must weigh
both sides. On the one hand, there is freedom of
movement, comfort, and safety. On the other hand,
there is expense, worry, and concern for the quality of
life. For many people in large cities, the reasons
against owning a car outweigh the reasons for owning
a car. Therefore, the answer is negative: A person in
an urban area should not own a car.[1]

Complete the following outline. Add more numbers
or letters to the outline if you need to.

Owning a Car
1. Reasons for
   a. move freely
   b.
   c.

2. Reasons against
   a. expense
      1. price of fuel
      2.
      3.
      4.
   b. worry and stress
      1. drive in rush-hour traffic
      2.
      3.
   c. pollution
   d.

This technique can also be applied to the students' own
writing. After they have written on an assigned topic, they
exchange papers and make an outline of each other's piece of

writing. If the writing is logically organized, they should be able to do the task without too much difficulty. If the writer has not been clear, however, then the outliner will be in trouble and will have to explain to the writer what is not working.

2. Ask the students to write a draft of a paragraph with a given opening sentence, such as, "With some English words, a knowledge of pronunciation does not help spelling at all." Then give them or write on the board a paragraph written on a related topic. A paragraph related to the topic above, for example, could be:

> There are some minor differences between American and British spelling. Where Britons end certain words with **-se,** Americans usually end the same words with **-ce** (British **practise** vs. American **practice**); the reverse is sometimes true, too (British **defence** vs. American **defense**). Notice also the British preference for final **-re** over the American **-er** (**metre** vs. **meter**). Finally, most Americans consider **neighbor** a correct spelling, but a Briton characteristically adds a **u** and spells the word **neighbour.**[2]

They work together to produce an outline of the paragraph:

> Topic sentence:
> There are some minor differences between American and British spelling.
>
> Support 1:
> British **-se** American **-ce**
> Example: **practise** / **practice**
> and so on.

Now they return to the draft of the original paragraph and see whether they can make an outline of what *they* have written. This activity helps students to look critically at their own writing and gives them ideas for revision.

3. Give students a reading passage that is clearly organized but above their reading level and therefore difficult for them. Ask them to read it quickly to get a sense of what is said and how it is organized. The following passage is challenging, but in spite of its difficult language, students are often delighted by the clarity and simplicity of the organizational design:

What I Have Lived For

Three passions, simple but overwhelmingly strong, have governed my life: the longing for love, the search for knowledge, and unbearable pity for the suffering of mankind. These passions, like great winds, have blown me hither and thither, in a wayward course, over a deep ocean of anguish, reaching to the very verge of despair.

I have sought love, first, because it brings ecstasy—ecstasy so great that I would often have sacrificed all the rest of life for a few hours of this joy. I have sought it, next, because it relieves loneliness—that terrible loneliness in which one shivering consciousness looks over the rim of the world into the cold unfathomable lifeless abyss. I have sought it, finally, because in the union of love I have seen, in a mystic miniature, the prefiguring vision of the heaven that saints and poets have imagined. This is what I sought, and though it might seem too good for human life, this is what—at last—I have found.

With equal passion I have sought knowledge. I have wished to understand the hearts of men. I have wished to know why the stars shine. And I have tried to apprehend the Pythagorean power by which number holds sway above the flux. A little of this, but not much, I have achieved.

Love and knowledge, so far as they were possible, led upward toward the heavens. But always pity brought me back to the earth. Echoes of cries of pain reverberate in my heart. Children in famine, victims tortured by oppressors, helpless old people a hated burden to their sons, and the whole world of loneliness, poverty, and pain make a mockery of what

human life should be. I long to alleviate the evil, but
I cannot, and I too suffer.

This has been my life. I have found it worth living, and would gladly live it again if the chance were
offered me.[3]

Ask the students to make a very brief outline of the material, for
example:

Topic: Three passions have governed my life.
1. Love
2. Knowledge
3. Pity

When students write their own compositions, they should be
encouraged to make similar brief outlines either orally or in
writing:

"My second paragraph is about . . ."
or
"My second paragraph says that . . ."

ANALYSIS

Outlining is just one technique to get our students to examine a
text—their own or somebody else's—closely. We can all learn a
great deal about how writing works if we concentrate not only
on *what* the writer has written but on *how* he has written it. If
we ask our students to analyze a reading passage, we are asking
them to ask questions about a piece of writing. This is an
extremely valuable aid to critical reading of one's own writing,
to revising, and to editing.

Examples
1. Give students a number of short paragraphs. Tell them that
you do not have time to read the paragraphs but that you will
read just *one* sentence of each. Ask them to decide, in pairs or
groups, which one sentence of each paragraph best expresses the
meaning of the whole. Which one will they give you? Why did
they make that choice?

2. Give or read students a paragraph with the topic sentence or the concluding sentence missing. You can then give students a choice of sentences to choose from, asking, "Which one did the writer use? Why did you make that choice?" If they are advanced students, they can discuss the passage and write their own sentence. For example, the paragraph on page 119 can be presented with the first sentence omitted. The students' task is to choose a sentence from these three:

a. British and American English are not the same.

b. There are some minor differences between American and British spelling.

c. The endings of British and American words are not the same.[4]

This type of exercise, too, is effective if done with the students' own writing. After a student has written, revised, and corrected a paragraph, he copies it onto the blackboard or paper, but omits the topic sentence. Other students then discuss what would be a logical sentence to insert. They compare their versions with the student's original sentence.

3. Give the students a short reading passage with a list of questions to analyze what the writer has done. Some sample questions might be:

• Which sentence states the main idea?

• Which sentences directly support that main idea?

• Has the writer used any listing words (**first, next,** etc.)?

• Which of the following did the writer do to support the topic: describe, define, divide into parts, compare, contrast, enumerate, explain, give reasons . . . ?

• How did the writer end the passage? What did the writer do in the ending—ask a question, summarize, introduce new material, point to future directions . . . ?

• Are any words repeated throughout the passage? Why do you think the writer repeats those words?

• How many parts would you divide this passage into?

Obviously, with a specific passage for study, questions relating more directly to the subject matter of the text can be devised.

4. Pictures provide an excellent basis for writing tasks where students can analyze and compare their methods of organizing ideas. If students all look at the same picture, the one on page 124 for example, and then write about it for a specific purpose, such as to describe to a family member the office where they have a temporary job, it will be interesting for them to compare the various ways in which they approached the task. They all had the same material to begin with, but how did they deal with it in their writing? Did they begin with the room or the people? How did they approach the layout of the room: ceiling to floor, front to back, right to left, or some other arrangement? How many details did they include and omit? Why did they choose to omit some? What was their opening sentence?

5. One of the main problems students have with organizing writing in English is in sorting out the differences between generalizations and specific details or between a topic and support. Sometimes they will write a series of unsupported generalizations, while at other times they will write a list of details and not make any kind of unifying statement about those details. They need practice in recognizing what they and other writers do. Look at the passages based on the picture on page 124:

a. Machines are as important to the office as people. The two telephones, the switchboard, the typewriter, the adding machine, and the photocopier save everyone a lot of time and effort.
b. There are a lot of machines in the office. On the receptionist's desk there are two: a telephone and a typewriter. To her right we see the switchboard. Behind the switchboard operator there is a photocopier, and the secretary behind the receptionist has a telephone and a typewriter.
c. The secretary has a typewriter and a telephone. The receptionist has a tidy desk. There is a photocopier on the table. The switchboard operator is a woman.

Discuss with the students what each writer has done. Have they all used specific details? (Yes.) Have they all formed a generalization from the details and have they expressed that in the

From the *Oxford Picture Dictionary of American English*,
p. 21. Copyright © 1978 by Oxford University Press, Inc.
Reprinted by permission.

form of a topic sentence? (Only in (a) and (b).) What point is (a) making? What point is (b) making? They describe the same details but what conclusions do they draw? Which passages seem more clearly organized? Why? Then discuss with the students in which other ways they could use details in the picture or support written generalizations about, for example, tidiness, spaciousness, efficiency, the difference from another office they know, or why they would or would not like to work there. The students write, exchange papers, and then describe which details their partner has used in support of which generalization. More advanced classes can extend the task to a topic that focuses not on the office in the picture but on office work in general. They can, for instance, write about why office work would be appealing to them or not.

6. A good way to get students to see and analyze the difference between a sentence that is simply a statement of fact (a supporting sentence) and one that makes a generalization that can then be developed and supported (a topic sentence) is to give them a pair of sentences such as:

  a. The cafeteria is very uninviting.
  b. The cafeteria is painted brown.

The students describe the picture each sentence produces in their mind. They ask the questions that each sentence initiates. They realize that Sentence 1 provides the writer with a chance to go on and write more and to answer the questions to show the reader precisely how the color of the paint, the lack of windows, the greasy tables, and the dirty floor all contribute to the impression that the cafeteria is uninviting. Sentence 1 makes us ask, "In what way?" After Sentence 2, we just say, "Oh" or nod. Exercises of this type can also be developed from the writing the students produce.

MODELS

Some textbooks present reading passages for students to analyze and imitate in their own writing. The students might read a pas-

sage comparing two bicycles, for instance, and then they write
their own composition comparing two cars, following the organization and structural patterns of the model as closely as possible. Or they might keep the same subject matter to write about
but vary the audience, the organization, or the purpose in their
own writing, such as when they rewrite a formal letter as an
informal one.

   The written model is not the only type of model. A model
of structure can be presented in a diagram, too, either for a paragraph as in

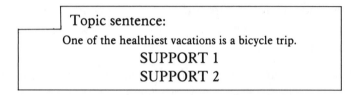

or for a longer composition as in

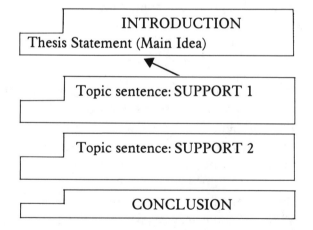

Models used in these ways produce, therefore, a kind of guided
writing.

   The problem with imitating these models, though, is not so
much that the task is guided but that the models themselves
encourage students to think that form comes first. They tend to
see the organizational plan of the model as a predetermined
mold (like a cake pan or a dessert mold) into which they pour

their content. But writing seldom works like that. We find the form to fit our meaning, not the other way around. The use of a model to initiate a piece of writing doesn't allow the writer to discover the shape that best fits the ideas he wants to express for a particular purpose.

We can avoid this rather mechanical use of a model if we employ it as "a resource rather than an ideal."[5] The student begins to write, gathering and shaping ideas rather than using given content or given form. He then utilizes a model not to initiate his own writing but to help him deal with a problem that emerges in the process of his own writing. He's not sure, for example, how it would be best to organize an argument—with the most convincing reason first or last? He can read, analyze, imitate, or manipulate a model as a way to throw light on the problem. As he sees how other writers deal with a similar dilemma, his own range of options increases. The model becomes not what he should do but only an example of what he could do.

Examples

1. After discussion and other prewriting activities such as brainstorming and listing, ask students to write about a topic, let's say about an early childhood experience. When they have written a draft, show them, for example, the passage on page 61. Ask them to list the points of information the writer provided, such as the details of time, place, and event. Then they return to their own writing to look at what they have done and to compare it to the model. They are not asked to make theirs like the model, simply to say where the two are similar and different.

2. The study of pairs of model passages can be illuminating if the passages are presented for the observation of a writer's choices and not for imitation. Let's imagine that the students are writing a composition about a decision they once made and the reasons for making that decision. They might well reach a point where they have chosen their focus and have made a list of reasons but they cannot decide how to organize their material. At that point, they could be given the two following paragraphs to read:

a.   There were several reasons why I decided to attend
      Bingston University. First of all, the tuition was rea-
      sonable. Second, the university had a deferred pay-
      ment plan; this represented a great convenience to my
      parents. Another reason was the fact that Bingston
      hires only the finest teachers. My chief reason, how-
      ever, was Bingston's mandatory work/study program in
      agriculture, my chosen field: the university requires all
      agriculture students to gain practical experience by
      working on farms in the area while they are still going
      to school; I knew that this would provide invaluable
      experience and prepare me to use the skills I had
      learned in the classroom.

b.   There were several reasons why I decided to attend
      Bingston University. My chief reason for choosing
      that university was its wonderful work/study program
      in agriculture, my chosen field. The university
      requires all its agriculture students to gain practical
      experience by working on farms in the area while they
      are still going to school; I knew that this would provide
      invaluable experience and prepare me to use the skills
      I had learned in the classroom. Second, Bingston hires
      only the finest teachers. Then, too, there was Bings-
      ton's deferred payment plan; this represented a great
      convenience to my parents. A final reason was the rea-
      sonable tuition.[6]

In the first passage, the reasons are arranged in ascending order
of importance, with the most important last. In the second, the
reasons are arranged in descending order. We need make no
judgment as to which is better. Only the context and the purpose
can determine that. It is enough that the students see that they
are different and produce a different emphasis. They then return
to their own writing with increased awareness.

3. A model passage can be used for restatement as well as for
analysis. The two passages used in (2) above can be used in the
following way:

Read passage (a) and discuss your answers to the fol-
lowing questions:
- What is the paragraph about?
- How many reasons does the writer give?
- Which sentences state a reason directly?
- Which ones tell us more about one of the reasons?
- Are the reasons arranged in any particular way?
What is the principle of organization?
- What other arrangements of the reasons would be
possible?

The students now work together on producing a paragraph that
contains the same material organized in a different way, according to a different principle of organization. They will not necessarily come up with exactly the same paragraph as (b), above,
as they could easily decide to use different devices to link the
ideas.

This type of exercise produces in students an awareness that
when they have generated some ideas, no immediately "correct"
pattern will emerge. The notes for the paragraph could be as
messy as this:

payment plan ⟩ REASONS ⟨ tuition
work/study program   teachers

Now the students have to decide how to organize the ideas with
the realization that there is not one right answer. What they
should be aware of is that they have options.

4. A chart, table, or graph can also provide a model for restatement, as in the following:

Directions: Below is a time line indicating some of the
events in the life of John F. Kennedy. Using the topic
sentence provided and the information on the time
line, write a paragraph in which you use chronological
development. Topic sentence: Kennedy's early career
foreshadowed the success he was to have as president.

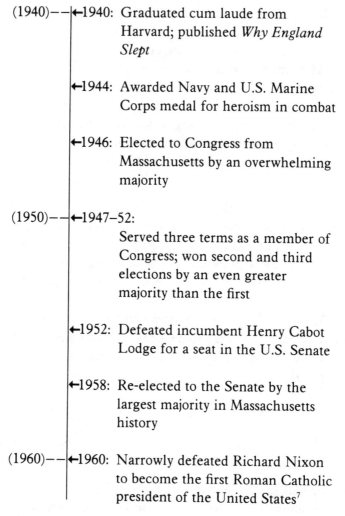

(1940)--|←1940: Graduated cum laude from
                 Harvard; published *Why England
                 Slept*

       ←1944: Awarded Navy and U.S. Marine
                 Corps medal for heroism in combat

       ←1946: Elected to Congress from
                 Massachusetts by an overwhelming
                 majority

(1950)--|←1947–52:
                 Served three terms as a member of
                 Congress; won second and third
                 elections by an even greater
                 majority than the first

       ←1952: Defeated incumbent Henry Cabot
                 Lodge for a seat in the U.S. Senate

       ←1958: Re-elected to the Senate by the
                 largest majority in Massachusetts
                 history

(1960)--|←1960: Narrowly defeated Richard Nixon
                 to become the first Roman Catholic
                 president of the United States[7]

Here the student's task is not to generate subject matter but to use the model of the notes to create a cohesive and unified piece of writing. Such a task can, of course, later be closely linked with a free writing task in which students will be using chronological order.

FROM MEANING TO ORGANIZATION

When people write outside the classroom, they never begin their thinking about their task like this: "I'll put the topic sentence first in every paragraph," "I'll write a description," or "I know, I'll write a comparison." They don't begin with form but with meaning. To give students the assignment to write a paragraph with a given topic sentence and with three supporting details is to deny the value of thinking through the topic to discover what the writer really has to say about it. What if he can only come up with two details? Is he to give up or frantically invent a third? Whenever possible, then, we should devise writing tasks so that when students write they are engaged in searching for the right organization for the ideas they want to express.

Examples

1. After looking at a picture or after hearing a word such as **beach**, students react by brainstorming, producing words and phrases as rapidly as possible. A typical list might be:

sand	sun	fish	seaweed
sea	suntan lotion	sleep	pool
blue	swim	seashell	sand castle
hot	ball		

Students look at what they have gathered and decide what to include, in what order, in a piece of writing for a travel advertisement to attract visitors to Margate Beach. They group the information and provide headings. During group discussion, students will have to justify and explain their categories. Let's say they come up with this:

Setting	**Activities**
sand	swimming
blue sea	playing ball
hot sun	sleeping in the sun
pools	fishing in the pools
shells	collecting seashells
seaweed	building sand castles

Now they can begin to see a possible shape for a piece of writing: two sections, one describing the place, the other detailing the variety of activities possible. Students can now work together to develop the sections and to provide a beginning.

2. More complex and more formal academic writing can be approached in a similar way. Students are given the beginning of a list; they add more examples to it. Then they arrange the items into categories and so uncover a scheme of organization, as in the following task:

> Add data to the following list, that is, enumerate more examples.
>
> **Methods of Transportation**
>
> 1. steamship   6. horse   11.
> 2. sailboat   7. jet plane   12.
> 3. bicycle   8. bus   13.
> 4. canoe   9. train   14.
> 5. automobile   10. propeller plane 15.
>
> Arrange the categories according to different methods of grouping.
> • 1st possible method of grouping: by kind of power used
> • 2nd possible method of grouping:
> • 3rd possible method of grouping:[8]

3. Scrambled paragraphs can be found in many textbooks. Students work together to decide which sentence comes first, second, and so on, until all the sentences have been used and the paragraph is completed with the sentences in logical order. Sentences can be in a book, on the board, or written on cards and distributed to the students, one sentence per student. In turn the students read out their own sentence when they think it is the appropriate place for the sentence in the paragraph. Textbook exercises like the following can be adapted in this way:

> Listen to the following information about Lincoln.
>
> a. When Lincoln was eight years old, his father lost most of his land in Kentucky.
> b. Lincoln's mother died when he was nine years old.

c. Lincoln's stepmother persuaded his father that Abraham should begin to go to school.

d. Lincoln was born in Kentucky.

e. He started school, but it soon closed.

f. The first winter they spent in Indiana they lived in a house with only three walls; the fourth side was open for a fire.

g. Lincoln was born on February 12, 1809.

h. A little more than a year later Lincoln's father married again.

i. Lincoln's family moved to Indiana from Kentucky.

j. Two years later Abraham went for a few weeks to another school.

The information about Lincoln above is not in logical chronological order. Read the sentences quickly to decide the order the sentences should follow.[9]

Students' compositions can also be presented to the class in the same way.

4. One student volunteers to describe a city or town that nobody else knows. As he mentions each place or building in the city, he puts a Cuisenaire rod (colored wooden rods of different lengths) or a children's play block down on the table or draws shapes on the blackboard to represent the size and position of the places. After he has described the city, the teacher describes it again, with help from the volunteer student or the class if he forgets anything or makes a mistake. Next, each student in turn points to a rod, block, or shape and says what he can about it. Then both the students and the teacher ask the volunteer questions about the city he described. After all of these language activities, with all the subject matter provided by the students, small groups form and the students write a description of the city, deciding whether to use the order of description that the student volunteer first presented or whether to change the order for better effect.[10] In an exercise like this, all the material—content and form—comes from the students. The organization grows out of the meaning.

· ACTIVITIES ·

1. Using the following excerpt from a textbook essay as a basis, devise classroom activities that will involve the students in outlining. Then make an outline of the passage yourself and compare your outline with another teacher's. Discuss any possible difficulties the students might run into.

A remarkable characteristic of American society is its diversity. For example, according to recent census reports, of the population of over 221 million, more than 16 percent were born in other countries or are the children of at least one foreign-born parent. They come from more than 17 European countries, as well as from Canada and Mexico and other Latin American nations. Almost 1.5 million are of Asian origin, particularly from Japan, China, and the Philippines. Over 22 million are blacks, and there are more than 700,000 American Indians (native Americans).

Approximately two-thirds of all Americans belong to a church. Of these, approximately 55 percent are Protestants, who are members of more than 70 different Protestant church groups. Almost 37 percent are Roman Catholic, and over 4 percent are Jewish. The rest are Moslems, Buddhists, Hindus, or members of other Christian churches.

Income distribution ranges widely. More than 36 percent of all American families have annual incomes of over $20,000. By contrast, almost 17 percent receive less than $7000.

Despite social and economic diversity among Americans, many American families have certain characteristics in common. Both the husband and wife were born in the United States and are of European ancestry. They have completed high school, and they are Protestants. Classified by income, they are middle class. The husband is employed and earns over $17,000 a year. They have an automobile, a television set, a radio, a washing machine, a refrigerator, and a telephone. They own their own home and spend about 50 percent of their income for housing and food. Clothing accounts for 6 percent of their expenditures, and medical care also amounts to 6 percent. Transportation, including maintenance and gasoline for their car, costs about 8 percent. Taxes account for almost 20 percent of their yearly expenditures. The rest of their income is used for such items as insurance, savings, gifts, and recreation.[11]

2. Find a passage in a textbook or magazine that would be useful in your classroom as a model of organization. Explain how you would use the passage. Pay particular attention to how students would apply what they learned to their *own* writing.

3. Taking as a basis either the passage in (1) above, or the passage you found for (2), devise classroom activities for students to analyze the organizational structure of the text. What instructions, for example, would you give for an assignment to differentiate between general statements and statements of support?

4. Find a picture and make up a writing assignment based on the picture. Consider what problems the students might encounter with organizing their piece of writing. What activities would you recommend to help them deal with those problems? It might be helpful to actually write the assignment yourself to see which organizational schemes *you* consider.

5. Find a reading passage, or use the one in (1) above, and scramble the sentences in two consecutive paragraphs. Write instructions for the students to reassemble the paragraphs. What do they need to look for in particular?

6. The students in your class have shown an interest in diet. One group's brainstorming session results in this list of ideas, just as the students produced them:

- A lot of people are vegetarians.
- Can you live on vegetables alone?
- You need some meat for protein.
- Protein is in a lot of foods.
- Meat can be fatty and fat is bad for you.
- A diet of grain, fruit, and vegetables is the best.
- But that's a boring diet.
- Some vegetables are better for you than others.
- It's not meat that causes problems—it's things like candy and ice cream.
- Are we talking about our health or our weight now?
- I'm going to eat whatever I want—I enjoy variety.
- Fish: why haven't we mentioned fish?

What would you ask the students to do next with this random list so that they move closer to finding a focus, exploring new directions, and organizing some material for a unified, cohesive piece of writing?

7. Brainstorm alone or with colleagues on how *you* would respond to the proposition on page 119 that "With some English words, a knowledge of pronunciation does not help spelling at all." Make notes and lists of your ideas, just as they occur to you. Make some order out of the chaos you have produced. How close are you to seeing a shape for a piece of writing?

8. Read the paragraph below and notice its clear pattern of organization:

> Houses that look exactly alike from the outside are often very different from each other inside. The Warren family and the Pepper family live on the same block in Brooklyn, New York, and their houses are

both very narrow, with four floors, two entrances, and six windows on the front. Yet inside there are four striking differences. Take the Warrens' house first. There are eight rooms, two on each floor, in addition to two bathrooms. Their kitchen is on the first floor at the back, with a view of the garden. The stairs are the original stairs of the old house, wooden and solid, and run up the side of the building. Their furniture is solid, too. They have a lot of antiques, such as big heavy desks, cabinets, and tables. The Peppers' house is different in every way. To begin with, they have only four rooms. Each floor of the house is one big open space, with a small bathroom on each floor. Their kitchen is on the second floor, since the first floor serves as the children's bedroom and playroom. In contrast to the Warrens' house, the stairs are metal spiral stairs in the center of the building. Also, the Peppers' furniture is anything but traditional. They have white modern furniture, and very little of it. In fact, most of the chairs and beds are just big pillows on the floor.

Topic Sentence:
Houses that look exactly alike from the outside are often very different from each other inside.

Support 1:
The Warrens' house
1. number of rooms: 8 and 2 bathrooms
2. position of kitchen: first floor
3. stairs: side, solid
4. furniture: antiques

Support 2:
The Peppers' house
1. number of rooms: 4 and 4 bathrooms
2. position of kitchen: second floor
3. stairs: central, spiral, metal
4. furniture: modern, white

Consider an alternative plan of organization that the writer of the paragraph might have used. Refer to Example 3 on page 129 and write a set of instructions for students to produce a restatement of the material, with the paragraph organized in a different way. Make an outline of the new paragraph that you predict the student will produce.

·CHAPTER NINE·

TECHNIQUES IN RESPONDING TO STUDENTS' WRITING

Responding to students' writing is very much a part of the process of teaching writing. It is not just tacked onto the end of a teaching sequence, a last chore for teachers and a bore for students. Rather, it is as important as devising materials and preparing lessons. More often than not, the sequence of classroom writing follows this common pattern:

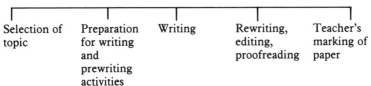

| Selection of topic | Preparation for writing and prewriting activities | Writing | Rewriting, editing, proofreading | Teacher's marking of paper |

In this case what the teacher says about the piece of writing can have no influence on the content, form, or accuracy of the piece. The teacher has spent all that time, but it is useless time! In the process line above, the teacher's response is to the finished product only. The teacher can only judge and evaluate, not influence the piece of writing. Responding to a paper only at the end limits us to doing the following:

1. giving the paper a grade (**A, B, C** or **70, 80, 90**, etc.);
2. writing a comment: **very good, needs improvement, careless;**
3. correcting errors.

If we sometimes feel the futility of this enterprise, let us put ourselves in the position of a student who has worked hard on a composition, looking up words in the dictionary, rereading, and checking. When he gets his paper back, it looks like this:

My family is a large family, having six people (live) together in the house. Each one has different way to help (them) relax. And also the way they thought is relaxing, having give me too much angry. ?

For example, my youngest sister (is love) chinese music, (therefor) whenever (she at home do her) homework always has the music on. That bother me a lot. Because she and I live in the same room (making) me

Selection of topic by teacher and/or students	Preparation for writing/ prewriting activities	Teacher reads notes, lists, outlines, etc. and makes suggestions	Student writes draft 1	Student makes outline of draft 1	Teacher and students read draft: add comments and suggestions about content	Student writes draft 2

have to stop with the arcurment with her. ?

   But the most angry is get up in the morning with ?

a disco music. That rely make me crazy. That whole

day I just have bad feeling. That is my youngest

brother relax's way.   to relax

What is the student to do now? What he does, of course, quite often is groan, put the paper away, and hope he'll somehow get fewer "red marks" next time.

   There are alternatives to this way of marking a paper. The teacher as sympathetic reader and editor can intervene at various points in the process. Our process line can look more like this:

Student reads draft 2 with guidelines or checklist: makes changes	Teacher reads draft 2: indicates good points and areas for improvement	Student writes draft 3	Student edits and proofreads	Teacher evaluates progress from draft 1 to draft 3	Teacher assigns follow-up tasks to help in weak areas

Such a process transforms a writing task from just "doing the assignment for the teacher" and trying to guess "what the teacher wants" to an interaction between writer and reader. Writing thus becomes more than a language exercise, marked **right** or **wrong.** It becomes an ongoing process of discovery. The paper above can be viewed by the teacher not as the final product but as the raw language material that the student is in the process of shaping. A response to the paper on page 140 as a first draft might look like this:

> You have told us about two members of your family. Now I am wondering what the others do to relax! Do they like music too? Read this aloud. If any sentences seem unclear, try writing them again. See if you can express the ideas in sentences 3, 4, and 8 more simply. Check the spelling of the three words I have underlined.

Before we look at specific techniques for intervening at various points in the writing process to respond to our students' writing, we can establish some basic principles that apply for all types of responses. My fundamental five are these:

1. When you pick up a student's piece of writing, don't immediately reach for a pen or pencil. Read the whole piece through first before you write anything. It is surprising how difficult it is for teachers to approach student writing unless they are armed with a pen.

2. Look for strengths as well as weaknesses, and let the student know what the strengths are.

3. If you use any editing symbols (**sp., cap.,** etc.: see page 152), make sure that the students are familiar with all of them and know what to do when they see one. Provide opportunities for the students to use the symbols, too.

4. Work out your own strategy for handling errors and explain it to your students. Decide if you will correct errors or simply indicate where they occur, if you will deal only with the errors you have discussed in class, with errors of a certain type, or with all errors; decide what importance you attach to grammatical errors and, again, let your students know.

5. Remember that when you or any other reader responds to a student's piece of writing, your main job is not to pass judgment on its quality (unless you are an examiner and not a teacher), but to help the writer see what to do next. Ask yourself: What should the writer do now to improve this paper? What does this paper need most?

With these basic principles in mind, let us now turn to some of the techniques teachers can use when responding to student writing.

WRITTEN COMMENTS

Comments on students' papers that take the form of a paraphrase of the ideas expressed, praise, questions, or suggestions are more productive than an end comment like "Only fair," "Good," or "Needs more work." What has been said of writers writing in their first language—"Noticing and praising whatever a student does well improves writing more than any kind or amount of correction of what he does badly"[1]—applies to ESL students, too. So our first task should be to read the paper through once first before writing anything on it and then to note what the student has done well, from organizing ideas to using the apostrophe correctly. After receiving praise of the strengths, the writer then needs to know what to do to improve the piece of writing. A suggestion to "Revise" tells nothing. Suggestions must be specific, giving directions that the student can follow, step by step. Questions are useful to us, too, if we want to lead the writer to consider other options without necessarily suggesting those options ourselves.

Examples

1. It takes a lot of time to mark all the errors in a composition and to explain what is wrong. In the following short piece of writing, we might mark, correct, and/or explain errors in verb form, use of the article **a,** and spelling:

> I got up at 8 o'clock this morning. Then I eated breackfast. At breackfast I ate an egg, a toast, butter, and coffee. After that I leaved my house.

Another way to use that marking time is to respond to the piece of writing as a whole with a supportive, helpful comment at the end, such as:

> You have written this very clearly. The punctuation of the list is correct. Try combining sentences 2 and 3 to avoid repetition of the word **breakfast.** Look closely at two forms you have used: **eated** and **ate.** Can they both be right?

When we have a large class with a lot of papers to mark and we need to be brief, we can respond in a similar, though briefer way:

> Very clear. Good punctuation. Now combine S 2 and 3. Check **eated** and **ate.**

If students are given the opportunity to revise in class, we can elaborate on our comments as we walk around the classroom. As the students look at their own work again and discuss it with other students and with the teacher, they might come up with the correct past tense form of **leave** as well.

2. Questions are valuable to direct a student's attention to unclear content or organization or to lack of details. Questions are implicit recommendations for revision:

> Ever since I was a small child the magic of tricks always were mysterious to me. One person who I believed was a master of it is Harry Houdini. He was the greatest and his magic will live on as the greatest. If I was to meet him at my magic dinner, all my mysteries would be answer. Maybe he will even teach me a trick to amaze my friends. I feel I'm the person who should find out the secrets that were buried with him.

Comment:
You have made me very interested in Houdini. What did he do that was so great? What mysteries do you

want to be answered? What exactly were the secrets that were buried with him? I'd like to know.

The student revised and improved on her first version, even correcting the faulty subject-verb agreement without being prompted. She added details and rearranged sentences. This is what she wrote:

> Ever since I was a child the magic of tricks always was mysterious to me. One person who I believed was a master is Harry Houdini. All his escapes from chains and jails shocked millions. His death in the water tank truly was a mystery. Some people think he did not know how to escape; others believe he suffered a bad cramp. I will find out at my dinner. I would like him to even teach me a trick to amaze my friends.

The student then admitted that she had just been to the library to check the facts and had found that Houdini had died of peritonitis. So she revised again.[2]

TALKING ABOUT THE PAPER

One of the best ways to help a student revise a paper is to discuss it with the student, in person. One-to-one conferences are extremely time-consuming and, in some teaching situations, just not practical. Often, however, a conference of just a few minutes can be so productive that some teachers hold very short conferences before and after and even during class while other students are writing or working together in groups. Talking to a student about what he has written is often the only way to find out what he was really trying to say. Some teachers have tried the technique of responding to students' papers by using a cassette tape recorder to record their responses.[3] This, however, provides only one-way communication. The virtue of the individual conference, however short it is, is that a real discussion takes place.

Examples
1. When we come across an obscure passage in a piece of student

writing, so obscure that we don't know what the student is trying to say, it is no help to write **?** or **awk** in the margin. Nor does it really help if we guess at the student's meaning and rewrite the sentence ourselves, especially if that is not the meaning the student intended. One teacher was faced with a passage like this in a student's account of an interview with another student to discover information about an important person in that student's life:

> Is good to know that someone always kept a good memory of someone close to and dear too. Sometime is not necessary to know a person visually. The legend of a person remain alive in many memories that one could picture the aquantance.
>
> As I made an interview of what individual is or had being more memorable to my interviewer that made me espression of knowing her la comadre (Godmother) the same length of time.

The teacher found it impossible to respond to the content of this piece of writing, so she talked to the student about it. He explained that he had been uncomfortable in the interview as he felt insecure about intruding in someone else's private family life. He then talked lucidly about the interview:

> "As I was interviewing this lady, she began to talk to me about her godmother and the relationship that assisted [existed] between godmother and godchild. The way she spoke about 'comadre'—the name she was known by in her community—was in a way that it makes me feel as if I have made her acquaintance before."[4]

He had, after all, a clear idea in his head, but he needed to feel that it was appropriate to express it. The obscure language was hiding meaning. Discussion of the passage was the only way for the teacher to discover the student's meaning and to help him out of his dilemma.

2. In a one-to-one conference, the teacher can ask the student to read a section aloud. Frequently the student will then spot errors like an unfinished sentence, a confused sentence, or an omitted word.

3. Some teachers, during a discussion about a topic with a student, make notes of what the student says. The student is then, in turn, surprised at the ideas produced in just a few minutes on a subject he thought he had nothing to say about. The teacher's written notes then form the basis for further prewriting activities.

CHECKLISTS

Teachers can use editing checklists and so can students. For grammatical items, checklists can be cumulative, with each new grammatical item covered in class added to the list. Checklists can contain questions about manuscript form ("Does your essay have a title?" "Is the first sentence of every paragraph indented?"), instructions about grammar ("Circle every pronoun and above it write the word or words in your composition that the pronoun refers to"), tasks to analyze content and organization ("Underline the sentence that expresses the main idea of each paragraph"), or just words to jog the memory ("verb forms").

Examples
1. A checklist can be very short and used first by the student to check a piece of writing and then by the teacher to evaluate it. A new checklist can be devised to fit each writing assignment, focusing attention on the critical features of one particular task:
- Which sentence expresses the main idea?
- Which sentences develop that main idea?
- Is every verb in the correct tense?
- Have you used the correct form of each tense?

Or we can use a simpler list:
- Main idea
- Supporting details
- Verb tense
- Verb form

This type of checklist focuses attention on form and grammar, without being overwhelming in its demands.

2. A checklist can be used to note only success with items that have been taught in class; the student gets a "plus mark" only when he has performed well on a particular item.[5] No negative marks are given. The idea is that, as the checklist forms a kind of syllabus of work covered in class, the number of plus marks will grow week by week.

STUDENTS' RESPONSES TO STUDENT WRITING

Checklists provide guidelines for students to read and assess other students' writing, and guidelines are valuable. Since teachers want their students to write a lot, and since they cannot read and mark huge quantities of writing, they have to find a means of enlisting the aid of other students in the class as readers. And, if students are alerted to what to look for and how to look for it, they can be very helpful to each other. It is not productive just to expect students to exchange and actually mark each other's papers. They tend either to say that the composition is very good or they mark everything wrong. With guidance, with clear, specific instructions on what to look for and what to do, they can be useful as readers of drafts.

Examples
1. In small groups of four or five students, each student reads his composition aloud. As he reads, he will very often notice sentences that are unclear or need grammatical correction.

2. Students form groups of three or four. They exchange their first drafts of compositions with another group. Each student in the group makes an outline of each essay he reads:

> Main idea: (copy sentence)
> Supporting points: 1.
>   2.
>   etc.

The students in the group compare their outlines and their perceptions of the composition. Then they give all the outlines to the writer of the piece, who now sees how readers view his work.

3. A student composition written on the board, shown on an overhead projector, or duplicated and distributed can be analyzed in whole-class or small-group discussion. What is good about the composition? What point is the writer making? List any generalizations the writer makes. What details support the generalizations? Students can look at each other's grammar, too, as long as they are given very specific guidelines, such as:

- Write down every verb that appears in the composition.
- Now write down the subject of each verb.
- Do subjects and verbs agree: singular subject/singular verb(-s)
                    plural subject/plural verb?

SELF-EDITING

What students really need, more than anything else, is to develop the ability to read their own writing and to examine it critically, to learn how to improve it, to learn how to express their meaning fluently, logically, and accurately. They need to be able to find and correct their own mistakes. All the techniques of reading closely and analyzing the writing, of course, help with critical reading. Some techniques are designed to help students apply the same critical skills to their own written products but at the right stage in the process. Right at the beginning of the process, as ideas are forming, they need to hold the critical skills in check. Students have to know not only how to edit their own writing but when is the right time to do it.

Examples

1. When students write a draft, they should concentrate on getting ideas down on paper. Encourage them not to worry about grammar and spelling (and if *you* don't, they are much less likely to). If they can't spell a word, they should just try it and put a question mark in the margin so that they can check the spelling later. If they don't know a word, they should feel free to write it in their first language and deal with it later. They should know that this draft is the first step and that nobody expects it to be perfect. Mistakes are totally acceptable in this context. Once they have some ideas down on paper, they can begin to group and regroup them, and deal with sentence accuracy as they progress from draft to draft.

2. Urge students to write a draft and then to put that draft away for a day or so before looking at it again. Then they read it aloud to themselves. Students report that when they do this, they often catch inconsistencies, muddled and incomplete sentences, omitted words, misspellings, and grammatical errors. Sometimes, teachers collect a composition draft and then deliberately keep it for two weeks and return it to the students unmarked. The students' job is then to look at their own work again with a fresher eye—the eye of a reader. Though the compositions are unmarked, this does not mean that they are unread. From first drafts, teachers make lists of problems that their students need to work on.

3. Encourage students to proofread by covering all the lines below the one they are reading and pointing at each word with a pencil.

4. Teach students how to use a dictionary and a grammar reference book.

5. Give students enough time to use checklists, read their work aloud, make an outline of their composition, refer to a handbook, and use a dictionary.

WAYS OF DEALING WITH ERRORS

While this book has been stressing that the teacher of writing has far more to do than simply correct errors, every composition teacher knows that errors in writing constitute one of the big problems of composition teaching. What is a teacher to do? Correct every error? But often that amounts to almost rewriting the student's whole paper. Correct some errors? But which? Not correct errors, but just indicate where they occur and let the student correct them? But if the student knew how to do it, wouldn't he have done it the first time? Ignore all the grammar errors and concentrate on content and organization? But then won't the student think that his grammar is acceptable and won't that reinforce the incorrect sentence patterns already established? All of these questions are of great concern to teachers of writing. Some basic principles for handling errors were listed on page 22. Specific techniques for classroom strategies in applying these basic principles are listed below.

Examples

1. With each set of student papers, don't try to mark all errors but decide which errors you will deal with. You might decide to mark only errors in grammatical areas taught in class. For one particular piece of writing, say one calling for the use of the future tense, you might decide to look only at how this tense is used. Or you might concentrate primarily on errors that make it difficult to understand the student's meaning, such as the wrong word order in the sentence "English language use much people." (The sentence also needs **many** instead of **much,** and **the** added before **English,** but neither of these errors interferes with communication as much as the faulty word order.[6])

2. Examine errors carefully. Try to determine the cause of the error: Is the student showing knowledge of a grammatical rule by overgeneralizing from it, by using **catched** on an analogy with **watched,** for instance? Careful analysis tells us a great deal about what the student knows (the regular past tense form) and what the student needs to know (irregular forms). It helps us plan our syllabus. Our next assignment in this case might be a guided composition in which a student writes a story in the past tense using given irregular verbs. The more we can point out to our students why they are making certain errors, the more they will be able to avoid them. Circling **assist** in the sentence "I assist my gym class every day" is nowhere near as helpful as letting the student know that he is using a cognate form (**asistir** in Spanish, which means **attend**).

3. Look for what the student has done correctly. Frequently, a piece of writing will contain forms both correctly and incorrectly used. The student needs to have it pointed out that he has demonstrated knowledge of the grammatical feature and has shown that he can use the correct form:

The lens must be adjusted. . . . A picture can be ruin by too much light.

4. Write down and duplicate student sentences that contain errors. Assign three sentences to each group in your class. Their task is to correct and improve their three sentences. Each group then reports to the whole class on how they repaired their sentences. Meanwhile, the writers of the sentences are all there, sitting in the room, hearing the suggestions.

5. Establish a set of symbols for indicating clearly identifiable errors. Use them when you know that the student is familiar with which grammatical rule to apply to correct the sentence. Here is a basic list of commonly used symbols:

¶ : start a new paragraph with indentation
sp.: spelling error
cap.: error in capitalization
p.: error in punctuation
v.: error in verb form or tense
∩ : change the word order ("She lost her key car.")
vocab.: wrong choice of word (**remind** for **remember**)
form: wrong word form (**efficient** for **efficiency**)
∧ : missing letter or word ("He tall.")
gr.: grammar error ("He have gone.")
SB: problem with sentence boundary: fragment or run-on sentence ("Because it was raining.")
SS: error in sentence structure ("He wants that I go.")

A teacher can point exactly to an error by circling or underlining it in the text and writing the symbol in the margin. Or, if the teacher only writes the symbol in the margin, then it is the student's task to figure out exactly where and what the error is.

6. As often as you can, provide a reason for careful editing and elimination of errors. Publication of a piece of writing where it will be read by others is one of the best motivating devices. Class magazines, letters, bulletin boards, and classroom walls provide ways of making writing public.

7. A final word: treat errors with seriousness and care and make sure your students do, too. But do not let concern for error dominate your writing class. If you do, you will be concentrating on the sentence and losing sight of the fact that we use sentences in sequence to express meaning, both in speech and writing. And expression of meaning is what we are aiming for in our language teaching and language learning.

· ACTIVITIES ·

1. Examine the following first draft of a piece of student writing. What are its strengths? What do you think is the main problem the student should work on in the next draft? Write a list of the grammatical structures the student has difficulties with. Discuss your responses with other teachers.

> When I was twelve years old and went to the 6th clase in my school, I had never read any books by Pushkin or other poets. Because I hate poetry, especialy those books which we had to learn in the class. I read a lot of autors, which we didn't studied in the school and a very few which we did. Of course I did not because of my lazy or something else; in this time, I thout, it was some sort of protest against the teacher of literature. My teacher was a very strong man and he was a real despot on our class. He never got us to think about the subject. He just wanted us to think right way. So his speach about literature and about poetry gave me a very negative exspretion.

2. You have to mark the composition above to return it to the student so that she can work on it some more. How would you mark it? With symbols, end comments, circling of errors . . . ? Mark it, and write a short paragraph explaining why you chose to mark it that particular way.

3. The student who wrote the draft above waits after class for a

ten-minute conference with you. She begins by asking, "Was my composition good?" How would you reply? What would you *do* in the conference? Outline your strategies.

4. Devise a checklist that a student could use to check and revise the first draft of the composition above.

5. Go back to the assignments you prepared for earlier chapters of this book. Choose three of them. Add to the materials and the instructions for each assignment some information about how the student should check his work for errors and explain what you will do about errors as you read this draft of the paper.

6. Prepare a checklist for the writer of the composition on page 140. Include in it what he should pay attention to in his next draft of this composition.

7. If you had decided to concentrate on getting the writer of the composition on page 140 to understand and correct *two* major errors, which two would you select? Why would you choose these two? Discuss your choices with another teacher. Then write directions for the student for activities that will help him work on these two types of errors.

·NOTES·

All books and articles are listed in the Bibliography, pp. 160–162.

NOTES FOR CHAPTER ONE

[1]For a full treatment of writing and learning, see Janet Emig, "Writing as a Mode of Learning."

[2]For examples of controlled compositions, see Linda Ann Kunz and Robert Viscount, *Write Me a Ream* and Christina Bratt Paulston and Gerald Dykstra, *Controlled Composition in English as a Second Language.*

[3]See Eugene Brière, "Quantity before Quality in Second Language Composition."

[4]See Robert Kaplan, "Cultural Thought Patterns in Intercultural Education" and "Contrastive Rhetorics: Some Implications for the Writing Process" and Elaine Dehghanpisheh, "Bridging the Gap Between Controlled and Free Composition: Controlled Rhetoric at the Upper-Intermediate Level."

[5]See Ann Raimes, "Composition: Controlled by the Teacher, Free for the Student" and *Focus on Composition* and Barry P. Taylor, "Teaching Composition to Low-Level ESL Students."

[6]See Keith Johnson and Keith Morrow, eds., *Communication in the Classroom* and Sandra McKay and Lisa Rosenthal, *Writing for a Specific Purpose.*

[7]See Barry P. Taylor, "Content and Written Form: A Two-Way Street" and Ann Raimes, "Anguish as a Second Language? Remedies for Composition Teachers."

NOTES FOR CHAPTER TWO

[1]The use of the information gap in the classroom is a feature of the communicative approach to language teaching. See particularly Keith Johnson and Keith Morrow, *Communication in the Classroom,* pp. 93–107.

[2]See, for example, Kenneth A. Bruffee, "Collaborative Learning: Some Practical Models."

[3]A variation on this technique, with students evaluating and ranking the compositions produced by the group, is discussed in Rebecca M. Valette, "Developing and Evaluating Communication Skills in the Classroom," pp. 416–17.

NOTES FOR CHAPTER THREE

[1]Useful picture sequences can be found in J. B. Heaton, *Composition Through Pictures* and *Beginning Composition Through Pictures,* Donn Byrne, *Progressive Picture Compositions,* Linda Lonon Blanton, *Elementary Composition Practice,* and L. A. Hill, *Writing for a Purpose.*

[2]Sets of class pictures that can be presented out of sequence are found in Linda Markstein and Dorien Grunbaum, *What's the Story?: Sequential Photographs for Language Practice.*

[3]For exercises using parallel pictures, see Ronald Ridout, *Write Now.*

[4]Figures from the 1980 Census.

[5]Adapted from Megan Webster and Libby Castañón, *Crosstalk: Book 1,* Chapter 11.

[6]Adapted from Donn Byrne, *Teaching Writing Skills,* pp. 85–87.

NOTES FOR CHAPTER FOUR

[1]A useful book for basic handwriting practice with forming the letters of the English alphabet is J. A. Bright and R. Pigott, *Handwriting.*

[2]For a full treatment of cohesive devices, see M. A. K. Halliday and R. Hasan, *Cohesion in English.*

[3]This technique is described in Mina P. Shaughnessy, *Errors and Expectations,* p. 142.

[4]This example is provided in William Rutherford, "Principled Sentence Arrangement," pp. 43–48.

[5]See Keith Johnson, *Communicate in Writing,* for various applications of this technique.

[6]From L. A. Hill, *Elementary Anecdotes in American English,* p. 44.

NOTES FOR CHAPTER SIX

[1]See James Britton et al., *The Development of Writing Abilities (11-18),* p. 88.

[2]Adapted from Keith Johnson and Keith Morrow, *Communication in the Classroom,* pp. 93–97.

NOTES FOR CHAPTER SEVEN

[1]See, for example, Linda Ann Kunz, *26 Steps* and Gay Brookes and Jean Withrow, *10 Steps.*

[2]From Gay Brookes and Jean Withrow, *10 Steps,* Demonstration Passage.

[3]From D. H. Spencer, *Guided Composition,* pp. 28–29.

[4]From Gloria Gallingane and Donald Byrd, *Write Away, Book 1,* pp. 94–95.

[5]Adapted from Ann Raimes, *Focus on Composition,* p. 28.

[6]From Lois Robinson, *Guided Writing and Free Writing,* p. 102.

[7]From Spencer, p. 49.

[8]See Frank O'Hare, *Sentence Combining.*

[9]See Patrick Kameen, "A Mechanical, Meaningful, and Communicative Framework for ESL Sentence Combining Exercises" and Vivian Zamel, "Re-evaluating Sentence Combining Practice."

[10]From Gallingane and Byrd, p. 98.

[11]Adapted from Heather Georgakopoulos and Robert Fertitta, *The International English Language Institute Writing Course Syllabus,* New York: Hunter College, 1981.

[12]This chart is reprinted by permission from the *IELI Writing Course Syllabus* by Georgakopoulos and Fertitta.

[13]Based on an exercise in Georgakopoulos and Fertitta.

[14]From Spencer, p. 13. Note that the population figures have changed since the passages were written.

[15]From Spencer, p. 50.

[16]See Christina Bratt Paulston and Gerald Dykstra, *Controlled Composition in English as a Second Language,* p. 16.

NOTES FOR CHAPTER EIGHT

[1]From Linda Lonon Blanton, *Intermediate Composition Practice: Book 1,* pp. 31–32.

[2]From Martin L. Arnaudet and Mary Ellen Barrett, *Paragraph Development,* p. 14.

[3]From Bertrand Russell, *The Autobiography of Bertrand Russell 1872–1914,* pp. 3–4.

[4]From Arnaudet and Barrett, p. 14.

[5]See Cynthia B. Watson, "The Use and Abuse of Models in the ESL Writing Class," p. 12.

[6]Adapted from Arnaudet and Barrett, pp. 48–49.

[7]From Arnaudet and Barrett, p. 96.

[8]From Mary S. Lawrence, *Writing as a Thinking Process,* p. 75.

[9]From Lawrence, p. 47.

[10]This is a version of a technique described by Earl W. Stevick, *A Way and Ways,* pp. 139–41.

[11]From Bertha C. Neustadt, *Speaking of the U.S.A.,* p. 165.

NOTES FOR CHAPTER NINE

[1]Paul B. Diederich, *Measuring Growth in English,* p. 20.

[2]From Ann Raimes, "Anguish as a Second Language?" pp. 267–68.

[3]See Mary Bracy Farnsworth, "The Cassette Tape Recorder."

[4]From Ann Raimes, *Problems and Teaching Strategies in ESL Composition,* p. 6.

[5]See Donald Knapp, "A Focused, Efficient Method to Relate Composition Correction to Teaching Aims."

[6]From Marina K. Burt and Carol Kiparsky, *The Gooficon,* pp. 6–7.

·BIBLIOGRAPHY·

Arnaudet, Martin L. and Barrett, Mary Ellen. *Paragraph Development: A Guide for Students of English as a Second Language.* Englewood Cliffs, N.J.: Prentice-Hall, 1981.

Blanton, Linda Lonon. *Elementary Composition Practice: Book 1.* Rowley, Mass.: Newbury House, 1979.

———. *Intermediate Composition Practice: Book 1.* Rowley, Mass.: Newbury House, 1981.

Brière, Eugene J. "Quantity before Quality in Second Language Composition." *Language Learning* 16 (1966), 141–152.

Bright, J. A. and Piggott, R. *Handwriting.* Cambridge: Cambridge University Press, 1976.

Britton, James et al. *The Development of Writing Abilities (11–18).* London: Macmillan Education, 1975.

Brookes, Gay and Withrow, Jean. *10 Steps: A Course in Controlled Composition for Beginning and Intermediate ESL Students.* New York: Language Innovations Inc., 1974.

Bruffee, Kenneth. "Collaborative Learning: Some Practical Models." *College English* 34 (1973), 634–643.

Burt, Marina K. and Kiparsky, Carol. *The Gooficon: A Repair Manual for English.* Rowley, Mass.: Newbury House, 1972.

Byrne, Donn. *Progressive Picture Compositions.* London: Longman, 1967.

———. *Teaching Writing Skills.* London: Longman, 1979.

Dehghanpisheh, Elaine. "Bridging the Gap Between Controlled and Free Composition: Controlled Rhetoric at the Upper-Intermediate Level." *TESOL Quarterly* 13, 4 (1979), 509–519.

Diederich, Paul B. *Measuring Growth in English.* Urbana, Ill.: National Council of Teachers of English, 1974.

Emig, Janet. "Writing as a Mode of Learning." *College Composition and Communication* 28, 2 (1977), 122–128.

Farnsworth, Mary Bracy. "The Cassette Tape Recorder: A Bonus or a Bother in ESL Composition Correction." *TESOL Quarterly* 8, 3 (1974), 285–291.

Gallingane, Gloria and Byrd, Donald. *Write Away: A Course for Writing English as a Second Language, Book 1.* New York: Collier Macmillan, 1977.

Georgakopoulos, Heather and Fertitta, Robert. *International English Language Institute Writing Course Syllabus.* New York: Hunter College, 1981.

Halliday, M. A. K. and Hasan, Ruqaiya. *Cohesion in English.* London: Longman, 1976.

Heaton, J. B. *Composition Through Pictures.* London: Longman, 1966.

———. *Beginning Composition Through Pictures.* London: Longman, 1975.

Hill, L. A. *Writing for a Purpose.* Oxford: Oxford University Press, 1978.

———. *Elementary Anecdotes in American English.* New York: Oxford University Press, 1980.

Johnson, Keith. *Communicate in Writing.* London: Longman, 1981.

Johnson, Keith and Morrow, Keith, eds. *Communication in the Classroom.* London: Longman, 1981.

Kameen, Patrick T. "A Mechanical, Meaningful, and Communicative Framework for ESL Sentence Combining Exercises." *TESOL Quarterly* 12, 4 (1978), 395–402.

Kaplan, Robert B. "Cultural Thought Patterns in Intercultural Education." *Language Learning* 16 (1966), 1–20.

———. "Contrastive Rhetorics: Some Implications for the Writing Process." In *Learning to Write: First Language, Second Language.* Eds. Ian Pringle, Aviva Freedman, and Janice Yalden. London: Longman, 1983.

Knapp, Donald. "A Focused, Efficient Method to Relate Composition Correction to Teaching Aims." In *Teaching English as a Second Language.* Eds. Harold B. Allen and Russell Campbell. 2nd ed. New York: McGraw-Hill, 1972.

Kunz, Linda Ann. *26 Steps: A Course in Controlled Composition for Intermediate and Advanced ESL Students.* New York: Language Innovations Inc., 1972.

Kunz, Linda Ann and Viscount, Robert. *Write Me a Ream.* New York: Teachers College Press, 1973.

Lawrence, Mary S. *Writing as a Thinking Process.* Ann Arbor: University of Michigan Press, 1972.

Markstein, Linda and Grunbaum, Dorien. *What's the Story: Sequential Photographs for Language Practice.* New York: Longman, 1981.

McKay, Sandra and Rosenthal, Lisa. *Writing for a Specific Purpose.* Englewood Cliffs, N.J.: Prentice-Hall, 1980.

Neustadt, Bertha. *Speaking of the U.S.A.* 2nd ed. New York: Harper & Row, 1981.

O'Hare, Frank. *Sentence Combining: Improving Student Writing without Formal Grammar Instruction.* Urbana, Ill.: National Council of Teachers of English, 1973.

Paulston, Christina Bratt and Dykstra, Gerald. *Controlled Composition in English as a Second Language.* New York: Regents, 1973.

Raimes, Ann. "Anguish as a Second Language? Remedies for Composition Teachers." In *Learning to Write: First Language, Second Language.* Eds. Ian Pringle, Aviva Freedman, and Janice Yalden. London: Longman, 1983.

———. "Composition: Controlled by the Teacher, Free for the Student." *English Teaching Forum* 16, 1 (1978), 1–7. Rpt. in *Readings in English as a Second Language.* Ed. Kenneth Croft. Cambridge, Mass.: Winthrop, 1980.

———. *Focus on Composition.* New York: Oxford University Press, 1978.

———. *Problems and Teaching Strategies in ESL Composition.* Arlington, Virginia: Center for Applied Linguistics, 1978.

Ridout, Ronald. *Write Now: Elementary Guided Composition through Pictures and Puzzles.* London: Longman, 1975.

Robinson, Lois. *Guided Writing and Free Writing.* 2nd ed. New York: Harper & Row, 1975.

Russell, Bertrand. *The Autobiography of Bertrand Russell 1872–1914.* London: Allen and Unwin, 1961.

Rutherford, William. "Principled Sentence Arrangement." *Mextesol Journal* 4, 4 (1980), 43–48.

Shaughnessy, Mina P. *Errors and Expectations: A Guide for the Teacher of Basic Writing.* New York: Oxford University Press, 1977.

Spencer, D. H. *Guided Composition.* London: Longman, 1967.

Stevick, Earl W. *A Way and Ways.* Rowley, Mass.: Newbury House, 1980.

Taylor, Barry P. "Teaching Composition to Low-Level ESL Students." *TESOL Quarterly* 10, 3 (1976), 309–320.

———. "Content and Written Form: A Two-Way Street." *TESOL Quarterly* 15, 1 (1981), 5–13.

Valette, Rebecca M. "Developing and Evaluating Communication Skills in the Classroom." *TESOL Quarterly* 7, 4 (1973), 407–424.

Watson, Cynthia B. "The Use and Abuse of Models in the ESL Writing Class." *TESOL Quarterly* 16, 1 (1982), 5–14.

Webster, Megan and Castañón, Libby. *Crosstalk: Book 1.* Oxford: Oxford University Press, 1980.

Zamel, Vivian. "Re-evaluating Sentence Combining Practice." *TESOL Quarterly* 14, 1 (1980), 81–90.

·INDEX·